Liverpool and Its Canal

by
Mike Clarke and Allison Hewitt

First published in 1992 by Merseyside Port Folios,
1 & 3 Grove Road, Rock Ferry, Birkenhead, Wirral, Merseyside L42 3XS.

Mersey Port Folios is the joint publishing imprint of the National Museums and Galleries on Merseyside and Countyvise Limited.

ISBN 0 9516129 3 X

Laser-printed by Northern Writers Advisory Services, Sale, Cheshire M33 4DN.
Printed by Birkenhead Press Limited,
1 & 3 Grove Road, Rock Ferry, Birkenhead, Wirral, Merseyside L42 3XS.

Acknowledgements

I would like to thank the staff of the many libraries and record offices I visited, particularly those at the Liverpool Record Office, the Maritime Record Centre, the Lancashire Record Office and my colleagues in the Local Studies Department of Lancashire Libraries. I also appreciated the help given by the staff of British Waterways, particularly Ian Selby and David Hayes. Liverpool City Engineers provided access to their extensive photographic collection in which several photographs of the canal, previously unpublished, were found. The Daily Post photo archives also produced "new" material. Other illustrations and information were provided by John Goodchild, Jack Parkinson, Philip Watkinson, members of NWSIAH and John Gibbons. My thanks are also due to Allison Hewitt and Adrian Jarvis for their part in producing the finished text.

Acknowledgements: Allison Hewitt

I would like to thank the members of the North West Society for Industrial Archaeology and History who walked the route of the canal and who researched some of the Industrial Archaeology for the book. Thanks also to Mike Chitty for providing me with useful snippets of information and to Nick Thorpe for reading and commenting on my draft text. Finally, thank you to Mike Clarke who has done all the hard work and whose book this really is, and to Adrian Jarvis for starting the project off and for pulling the whole book together at the end.

CONTENTS

Merseyside Port Folios

Merseyside Port Folios is a joint imprint of the Trustees of the National Museums and Galleries on Merseyside (NMGM) and Countyvise Ltd, set up to produce a series of occasional booklets on subjects in the history of Merseyside's Dockland.

The work is being done by the Port Survey, a small research unit within the Merseyside Maritime Museum which operates with substantial financial assistance from the Merseyside Development Corporation. Its key responsibilities are to assess the historical importance of sites and buildings within the MDC's Designated Area, to ensure that anything of importance is adequately researched and recorded, and to publish the results wherever these may appear to be of reasonably general interest. The booklets are intended to be accessible and "readable" whilst retaining quite extensive bibliographies and notes for the scholarly user.

The task of producing the first two booklets proved easier than expected in some respects, but more difficult in others. It was easier in that the enormous archival resources of NMGM reduced the amount of field recording and measurement needed by furnishing contemporary descriptions, and often drawings, of virtually everything surviving on the ground.

This Port Folio is quite different from those which have preceded it and those which are to follow. Quite clearly, the industrial corridor which formed alongside the Leeds and Liverpool Canal was a significant component in the history of the northern part of the Merseyside Development Corporation's Designated Area. It was, however equally clear that it would be fairly pointless for staff of the Port Survey to attempt to write this booklet when Mike Clarke had been working on the history of the canal for about ten years and was just about to finish his considerable book. Equally, it would be foolish for us to try to gaze into our crystal ball as to what might happen to the canal in the near future when Allison Hewitt is employed specifically to look for a useful future for the remainder section of the canal. We could have gone towpath-walking, but there is a small cadre of members of the North Western Society for Industrial Archaeology and History who enjoy doing this, one of whom was actually involved in a scheme to improve part of the area bounding the canal until his then employer (Merseyside County Council) was abolished.

The Port Survey, therefore, has mainly acted as an enabling agency for this booklet. I have undertaken the editing, some of the picture research and the index, Samantha Ball has done the line illustrations and Sandra Page has, as ever, sorted out the textual disasters and the awful handwriting to the point where the typesetter could understand them. Colin Pitcher did the site photography, and David Flower of NMGM and John Calderbank of City Engineer's Reprographic Section produced the prints from numerous historic negatives in their respective charges.

1
A Need And A Beginning

At the start of the eighteenth century Liverpool was emerging from being a minor port serving trade with Ireland. Many factors led to the development of the town as England's fastest growing port: its geographical location on the west coast, ideally suited for trade with the increasing colonial markets in America and Africa; the entrepreneurial skills of its merchants; and perhaps most important, the arrival of Thomas Steers in 1709 to construct the town's first dock. Steers was not just Liverpool's first Dock Engineer, but was also involved in the political and economic life of the town.[1] The dock which he built, the first commercial dock in the country, allowed ships to be loaded and unloaded with greater security and with less interference from the weather than hitherto. However, it was his realisation of the importance and his encouragement of transport links with the town's hinterland which was to lay the foundation for Liverpool's success.

Less than three years after Steers' arrival in the town he had produced two surveys for river navigations, one up the Douglas to Wigan, the other up the Mersey and Irwell to Manchester. In these plans he was probably ahead of his time as they were not completed until 1742 and 1736 respectively. Before his death in 1750 he had undertaken work on the Calder and Hebble in Yorkshire, built the Newry Canal and surveyed the Boyne Navigation in Ireland, besides being involved with the turnpike from Liverpool to Prescot. The Town Council, too, soon realised the importance of inland transport and Steers' successor, Henry Berry, was allowed time off from his duties as Dock Engineer to build the Sankey Navigation, opened in 1757, from Warrington to the St. Helens coalfield. The Council had previously been involved with the Weaver Navigation, and, following the success of the Duke of Bridgewater's Canal at Worsley, granted money towards the cost of surveying two proposed canals, the Grand Trunk (Trent and Mersey) and the Leeds and Liverpool.

The Promotion of the Canal

The proposal for a canal linking Leeds with the Irish Sea had first been raised in the *York Courant* on 7th August 1764. Initially it was the merchants and coal-mine owners of Bradford, headed by John Stanhope, who took up the suggestion. They were anxious to increase their supply of lime, used both as a fertiliser for the improvement of agricultural land, and for mortar and decoration in building work. In West Yorkshire much was obtained by burning limestone from Craven with coal from local mines. An earlier unsuccessful plan to make the River Aire navigable to Skipton, in 1743, was proposed for the same reason. Besides this local traffic in lime, they hoped that a canal to Liverpool would enable them to increase the export of locally produced woollen goods to the expanding colonial market in America. The Yorkshire men called a meeting in Bradford in 1766 to promote the scheme and over one hundred subscribers paid towards the cost of making a plan and estimate. This was undertaken by John Longbotham who presented his initial survey to the promoters at a meeting in Bradford on 7th January 1768,[2] where it was suggested that the canal should also be promoted in, and subscriptions obtained from, Lancashire.

The merchants in Yorkshire, who had long been exporting woollen goods to Europe, were well established with secure finances. This enabled them to organise the promotion of the canal relatively easily. In Lancashire, industry was yet to advance far beyond the production of goods for the local market. Only in Liverpool, where the colonial trades were rapidly increasing, were many merchants able to finance such a project. As a result interest in the canal was slow to develop in Lancashire, though the Corporation of Liverpool took the initiative in suggesting that James Brindley should survey the scheme.[3] They had already given £200 towards the cost of the first survey and now offered a further £50 towards Brindley's fees. A meeting was eventually held at Preston on 25th August 1768 when a committee of forty gentlemen was nominated.

A joint meeting of the two committees, from Lancashire and Yorkshire, was held in Burnley in December 1768 when it was agreed to apply to Parliament in the following session, so there was a year's wait during which some of the Liverpool promoters became unhappy about the route, proposing instead a line through Wigan. Their motive was coal.

A Compromise Over The Route

The Yorkshire promoters, as mentioned above, desired a canal for two reasons: to improve the supply of lime and limestone from Craven to the Bradford district and for their woollen goods to reach the colonial market through Liverpool. To achieve this their proposed line went up the Aire valley to the Craven limestone district, from there to Padiham and then directly to Liverpool.

This plan was opposed by the Liverpool promoters who demanded a canal which would give them a regular and cheap supply of coal. Throughout the eighteenth century Liverpool was an important industrial centre where pottery, chemicals, sugar, salt, copper and many other products were manufactured or refined.[4] It was only when land prices and wages became significantly higher than in neighbouring areas of Lancashire, and when problems with pollution increased dramatically, that the town ceased being Lancashire's industrial centre. The Sankey Navigation and its proprietors had been supplying these industries with coal since 1757, and their virtual monopoly allowed them to raise prices. By providing a second source of coal for the town, the Liverpool merchants hoped that the Leeds and Liverpool would reduce the price and increase the availability of coal. To do this the canal had to pass through a suitable coalfield so the Liverpool promoters produced a scheme for the canal which passed through the Douglas Valley to the coalfields of Wigan and Chorley, Yorkshire being reached via Blackburn and Burnley.

The ensuing battle between the two groups was bitter, but through the arbitration of John Hustler of Bradford a compromise was arranged.[5] The Yorkshire promoters' line was chosen but the canal would be built from either end simultaneously, which allowed both groups to achieve their main aims quickly; limestone would be available from Craven for Bradford and coal could be brought from Wigan, via the Douglas Navigation, to Liverpool. The main line of the canal was to pass through the sparsely populated area north of Blackburn, and it was not until 1793 that the present route through Burnley to Wigan was substituted.

The Douglas Navigation

The Douglas Navigation, which gave boats access to Wigan, had been built by Alexander Leigh, a Wigan attorney, and opened in 1742. By 1770 it carried about 12,000 tons of coal annually, mainly for the Irish market, though many ports on the Lancashire coast, including Liverpool, were also served. Other cargoes carried included ashes and kelp for soap manufacture, potatoes, grain, and, that most important eighteenth century commodity, limestone. The coal and cannel brought by the Navigation from the Douglas Valley were of top quality and sold for higher prices than other coal. Cannel burnt with a bright flame, leaving little ash, which made it very suitable for household use. Later it became the main fuel used in Liverpool to produce coal gas when works were established in 1815.

Initially, Alexander Leigh had opposed the canal scheme as he was worried about the proposed aqueduct over the Douglas at Parbold restricting the size of boat capable of using his navigation. Clauses were inserted in the Canal's Act to protect the Navigation below, the most important being for a link from the canal at Parbold to the river at Dean, near Gathurst. It was this which would allow Liverpool to be supplied with coal from the Wigan area. By 1771 Leigh had suggested and agreed to the sale of the Navigation to the Canal Company, so the link to Dean was built by the Canal Company and the Navigation became part of the canal route. Despite this, it was still known as Leigh's cut. There was one lock on this length, at Appley Bridge, which was built large enough to allow boats 74 feet long by 14 feet 6 inches wide to pass and dictated the size of boats used on the canal into Liverpool.

The Canal is Opened

After agreement over the choice of route had been reached by the Lancashire and Yorkshire promoters, an Act was quickly obtained and the work of construction commenced in 1770. Unfortunately the estimated cost was found to be extremely optimistic. The company was only able to afford to build the sections from Leeds to Gargrave, opened by 1777 and from Liverpool to the Douglas Navigation at Dean, opened in 1774. However, as these sections allowed limestone to reach Bradford and coal to reach Liverpool, neither groups of proprietors were unduly worried and it was not until 1790 that they again began to think about connecting the two sections of the canal.

The only additional work undertaken before then was the elimination of the old Douglas Navigation which had fallen into a very dilapidated state.[6] The way this was done shows that there were still considerable differences between the Lancashire and Yorkshire committees. Work was started by the Lancashire men on the section from Dean to Wigan, with their maintenance engineer, Robert Dickenson, in charge. The locks on this length were built to the same size as at Appley Bridge, as boats had already been built to these dimensions. The canal from Burscough to Rufford, however, was built by the Yorkshire committee's engineer Richard Owen, with locks of the same size as those in Yorkshire; 62 feet long by 14 feet 6 inches wide. It seems absurd that such a situation should occur, the only explanation being the stubbornness of the Yorkshire men, who had a controlling interest in the canal.[7] Their obduracy continued into the nineteenth century. When the Leigh Branch was opened in 1820 the locks were built to the Yorkshire size, despite linking with the Bridgewater Canal which accommodated 70 foot long boats. It was only after Pickfords complained, in 1820, that their 70 foot narrow boats could not reach Liverpool that the locks from Leigh to Wigan were enlarged to match those from Wigan to Liverpool. To the east of Wigan the locks could only take Yorkshire sized boats, 62 feet in length.

The Boats

The Sankey Navigation, opened in 1757, was built to take boats 68 feet long by 16 feet 6 inches wide, which allowed a typical coastal trading vessel or flat to pass. Locks on the Douglas Navigation were slightly narrower and could only be used by estuarial craft, which were smaller. On the Leeds and Liverpool, in Lancashire, the locks were built to suit the latter type of boat, though they were made long enough to accommodate the new narrow boats, only 7 feet wide, which had been developed on the Bridgewater Canal. Such boats were easy to build and had been used during the construction of the Lancashire section. They were subsequently sold for use by traders on the canal and could carry from 15 to 18 tons.[8] It seems likely that these boats were only used while traffic was sought initially and that as trade increased new wide boats were built to suit the locks. Many of these had square sterns, similar to the flats working on the Mersey and could carry about 35 tons. To increase

Typical Leeds and Liverpool horse boat and crew. Authors collection.

the speed at which boats passed through locks the round stern was grad-
ually adopted, as this enabled the boatman to start shutting the lock-
gates before the boat was fully into the lock.

Boats on the Douglas Navigation had been hauled by men, but when
the Leeds and Liverpool was built a tow-path was provided which enabled horses to be used instead though manpower was used initially.[9]
Sailing boats delivered coal from Wigan to Liverpool after 1820, but
they were towed along the Leigh branch and Bridgewater Canal, then
sailed down the Mersey estuary. It was only after a link was built from
the canal to Stanley Dock, in 1846, that sailing flats may have appeared
on the canal in Liverpool. Even then their masts would have to be lowered and they were towed by horse to their destination. Dumb boats
were preferred, as they could pass more easily through Great Howard
Street bridge at the entrance to the canal. Steam driven tugs were introduced from the eighteen-fifties on the Wigan coal traffic, but it was not
until the eighteen-eighties that steam was used for merchandise boats.
Single and twin cylinder diesel engines were fitted from the nineteen-
twenties, eventually becoming the usual method of propulsion.

There were two main types of canal boat, those for carrying minerals
and manure, and those for grain and merchandise. The holds of the for-

Stanley Dock in 1990. Access to the canal was via the bridge under Great Howard Street in the centre distance. The headroom under this bridge restricted the size of boat which could reach the canal. Author's Collection.

mer were left open to the weather, while to keep the latter dry, sheets and coamings were provided.[10] Living accommodation for the boatmen and their families was provided in cabins at the bow and stern. Although some families did live on board, the majority had a house ashore. Many boatmen came from the West Lancashire canalside villages, particularly Burscough, though a few came from Liverpool, often living in houses near the Bootle canal depot.

The Canal and Liverpool's Development

Following the opening of the canal in 1774, trade increased rapidly. Many canal proprietors, from both Liverpool and Yorkshire, invested in the Douglas Valley coal mines, their money enabling these mines to be enlarged. 12,000 tons of coal had been sent down the Douglas in the years prior to the opening of the canal. This traffic increased marginally but was soon overwhelmed by the tonnages sent to Liverpool. By 1780 almost 36,000 tons were delivered, and this had increased to over 137,000 tons ten years later,[11] more than ten times the tonnage of merchandise carried. Industry, which had previously been located near the docks, was soon attracted to the canal by this plentiful supply of coal, and chemical, glass and brick works were erected alongside. The canal also provided safe and smooth transport for people; packet boats operated between Liverpool and Wigan almost from the day the canal opened.[12]

The terminal basin at Old Hall Street was regularly enlarged to cope with increased traffic, but no other major work was undertaken on the Lancashire section of the canal in the eighteenth century apart from bypassing the Douglas Navigation. Money to begin completion of the canal was eventually raised in the seventeen-nineties, with work starting on the Yorkshire end. Progress was slow and finance precarious; much of the canal's profit had to be put towards the new works, to the detriment of dividends. There were further conflicts over the route, particularly with the Lancaster Canal, but a compromise was finally reached and the canal opened from Liverpool to Leeds in 1816. Four years later the Leigh branch was completed, linking Wigan with the Bridgewater Canal and forming a route from Liverpool to the midlands and the south. The only outstanding part of the original scheme was a link to the river, and this was to take a further twenty-six years to complete.

From 1816 the canal had a virtual monopoly on trade to East Lanca-shire and a dominant hold on Liverpool's coal supply. This was short lived, as fourteen years later the Liverpool and Manchester Railway op-ened. Trade with Wigan, Leigh and Manchester was affected, but it was not until the East Lancashire Railway entered Liverpool in 1848 that the canal's main traffics began to be challenged. After two years of severe competition an agreement was reached, in 1850, for merchandise traffic on the canal to be leased to a group of railway companies for twenty one years, later extended by a further two years. This gave the canal com-pany a guaranteed income and though the railways siphoned off traffic, it enabled the canal to build up its financial reserves. These were then used to improve the canal's facilities when the lease was given up and enabled the canal to compete effectively with the railways in the latter part of the century.

There had always been considerable traffic with the docks, goods being carried to and from the canal basin by horse-drawn lorries. A link to the docks would have overcome the inconvenience of transshipping, and this had been proposed in the canal's first Act. It was finally achieved in 1846, seventy-six years later, when a branch was built to the new Stanley Dock although the latter was not formally opened until 1848. This at last enabled goods and coal to be interchanged without the use of road transport.

During the nineteenth century many of the manufacturing industries on the canal banks disappeared, though they were replaced by service industries, such as gas works and warehousing, which resulted in a con-tinual increase in the traffic carried during the century. However, tolls fell with railway competition, and this adversely affected the dividend paid to shareholders. In an effort to improve matters following the sur-render of the railway lease in 1873, considerable amounts of money were spent on new warehousing, particularly in Liverpool and Bootle. The company also built up their own fleet of boats for the carriage of merchandise and towards the end of the century were taking traffic away from the railways,[13] especially the Lancashire and Yorkshire.

Unfortunately their success was part of their downfall. There had been long running complaints from coal owners over compensation for coal left under the canal to stop subsidence, and from local government over the canal's low rateable value, which were only overcome by substantial payments from the company. The Railway and Canal Traffic Act of 1888, which limited tolls, also had the effect of reducing income to a canal already short of cash because of its improvement scheme. The First World War brought further financial difficulties as canals were treated less favourably, with respect to Government compensation, than railways.[14] Much proposed canal improvement had to be abandoned. In the nineteen-twenties and thirties, the introduction of the lorry and the decline of traditional industries on which the canal had relied, were the precursor to the end of carrying. A large volume of traffic continued only because industries using coal continued to be supplied by canal. Tate and Lyle and the gas works at Linacre and Athol Street, the last major users of canal transport, were served into the nineteen-sixties, but the severe winter of 1963 and the decline in the quality of coal from Wigan finally brought about the end of trade on the canal.

Delivering coal to Tate & Lyle.

2
The Canal Terminal

By the mid-seventeen-sixties Liverpool was one of the country's major ports, with almost a thousand ships leaving every year.[15] The Old Dock and the Salthouse Dock had already been built, with Georges Dock and Dukes Dock soon to open. Industry was developing: the manufacture of pottery, soap, ironwork and glassware, and the processing of salt, copper and sugar were well established, while the importation of cotton was beginning, though few textile mills were ever erected in the town. Having direct links with the trade of the port, these industries tended to be along the river front, and consequently wealthy residents were beginning to move out of the town centre to the less developed high ground to the east. It was into this rapidly changing environment that the Leeds and Liverpool proposed to enter.

Land was always cheapest away from town centres, which were consequently avoided in constructing the Leeds and Liverpool. Subsequently, as industry developed because of the improved services provided by the canal, the towns expanded outwards to encompass it. This happened in Liverpool where the canal entered from the less developed north, though here Lord Derby demanded higher prices than for his land elsewhere on the canal,[16] an indication of the pace of expansion in the town, rather than of his rapacity.

For the town's merchants, the canal's main purpose was the supply of coal; not just for industrial and domestic use, but also for export, particularly to Ireland. The market for coal was enormous; in 1794, twenty years after the canal had opened, over 150,000 tons were being delivered annually, and several of the canal's proprietors had become coal owners and merchants, with their mines located in the Douglas Valley near Wigan. The effect on the town was immediate, with industry developing on land owned by the canal company between Vauxhall Road and Love Lane.[17] Because of the improved services which the canal provided, land in this area was to rise in value, becoming too expensive for housing. Thus the canal came to dominate the development of the northern side of the town for many years, with effects on land use which are clearly visible to this day.

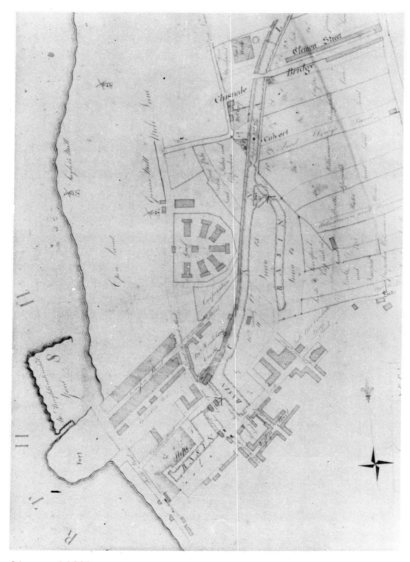

Liverpool 1802.

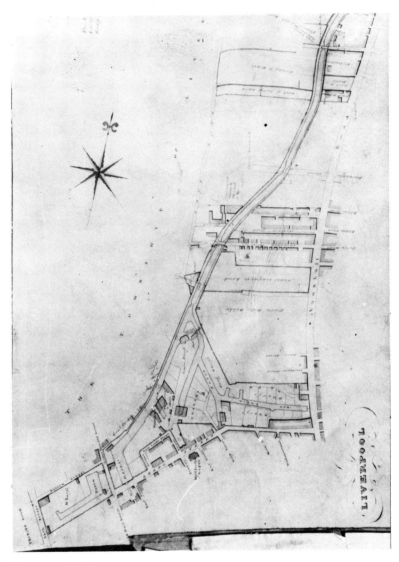

Liverpool 1827.

The Original Basin

At first the canal's terminal basin was on the edge of the town, at the end of Old Hall Street. Princes Dock was not to be built for almost fifty years and townsfolk took the air on "Ladies Walk", an avenue lined with elm trees, which ran down to the river from Old Hall Street. Alongside the river were the sea water baths, erected in 1765, from which Bath Street took its name. These were used by the wealthy while ordinary folk resorted to the beach to the north. Before the pollution caused by the widespread use of water closets and the sewer "improvements" they made necessary, this use of the river was much less repugnant than might be imagined. Back on the canal there were coal wharfs on the east side of the basin, merchandise being handled from a wharf on Old Hall Street. A dry-dock for repairing boats was available a few hundred yards from the end of the canal, and a gauging dock to ascertain how much each boat would carry so that the correct toll could be charged, was built nearby.

By 1790 trade had increased to such an extent that an enlargement of the facilities at the basin was needed. A link to the river had always been part of the original plan but had never been built. The idea was raised again by the Dock Committee, while the canal company preferred a waggonway with shoots.[18] Agreement could not be reached, and instead further coal wharfs were provided by extending the basin in 1792. Ladies Walk was purchased, and the basin extended to Bath Street, with five new coal wharfs in Dutton Street. Old Hall Street crossed the entrance to this basin by a hump back bridge flanked by Canal Company offices. A further office was provided in Old Hall Street for the coal companies. It is now a listed building incorporated in St. Paul's Eye Hospital, being the only building remaining from this period of the canal's history.

The area around the basin was becoming increasingly built up: Leeds Street, named after the canal, opened about 1790, shortly after Gibraltar Row and Dutton Street were laid out. Great Howard Street,[19] originally Mill Street as it led to Mr. Green's and Mr. Taylor's windmills, was extended, receiving its name from the philanthropist John Howard who was involved with the erection of the new town gaol in 1786, near to the basin.

Merchandise traffic was increasing, though it never really flourished until the canal was opened throughout in 1816.[20] Two warehouses were provided for its accommodation, one for the traffic to Wigan and a second for the Preston trade. This used the branch from the canal at Burscough down to the River Douglas at Sollom, reaching Preston by the Ribble estuary. It provided a safer and more regular route for goods than by trusting to the vagaries of the tidal passage around the coast. Warehousing was also provided by merchants in the surrounding streets where many also had their houses. The opening of the canal brought major changes to this area as industry and commerce thrived. The merchants slowly moved to more refined districts in the east and south of the town, away from their warehouses, though the Blundell-Hollinsheads, a merchant family who had large interests in the canal, remained in the district until 1820.

Trade and Extensions

As traffic increased so did pressure on water space. Another arm of the canal was built on the east side of the existing basin in 1800 for the use of the timber trade, and a second arm, built between 1808 and 1810, extended the basin system to Vauxhall Road. Clay underlies much of the land to the north of the town, and all that was excavated in building these arms was sold to local brick-makers. Their works were often adjacent to the canal where coal was easily available for firing the bricks.

The basin area was a hive of activity. Besides brick-making and the timber yards, coal yards were operated by Mr. Clarke, Mr. Blundell, Peckover and Co., Hustler and Co. and several others, many of whom were both canal proprietors and coal owners with mines in the Douglas Valley. A rope-walk was erected opposite the dry-dock, convenient for supplying boatmen, and a white lead works had opened around 1800 just beyond Chisenhale Street Bridge. The Bootle Waterworks, one of two private companies which provided the only supplies of water to Liverpool until 1847, were located to the east of the basin in an area known as Pumpfields. Public services were also represented by manure wharfs, and for many years the town's refuse was removed by boat for use as fertiliser, particularly on land reclaimed by the draining of Martin Mere in West Lancashire.

The canal was opened through to Leeds in 1816. This led to an increase in traffic, the Union Company of carriers transferring its Yorkshire trade from the Rochdale Canal, which had opened from Manchester to the Calder and Hebble Navigation in 1804. Four years later in 1820 the opening of the Leigh branch joined the Leeds and Liverpool to the rest of the canal system. Pickfords were soon using the canal for a narrowboat service from the midlands and occupied a warehouse at the basin for a short while. However, the long journey via Manchester and Leigh was inconvenient and they soon gave up, their cargoes being transshipped into flats at Runcorn for delivery via the tideway to Liverpool, a much shorter passage. Other large carriers included Kenworthy's who used the canal until 1842, when they gave up their warehouse following the introduction of railways. There were further extensions to the basin system in 1825, when a short arm was built towards Leeds Street, and in 1839 when an arm was built towards Vauxhall Road, parallel to Charters Street. This formed the maximum extent of the canal basin network, by which time over £60,000 had been spent on the wharfs, warehouses and offices. The main offices for the canal were originally in Bradford which had provided much of the initial impetus for its construction. By 1850, however, trade in Lancashire was more important and,[21] following the promotion of Mr. Tatham from the Liverpool office to General Manager, the main offices were moved to Liverpool.

Social Conditions

By the middle of the nineteenth century the town's population was soaring. It had increased from under 50,000 in 1785 to 222,954 by 1841, and, with the growth of Irish immigration, sanitary conditions were becoming a problem. This was particularly so in the Vauxhall and Exchange Wards which encompassed the canal basin. Although few boatmen lived in Liverpool, being generally from the small towns and villages along the canal in West Lancashire, there were many people relying on the canal for employment who lived near the basin. Among these were the coal heavers who unloaded the boats. Working in gangs of four, each gang unloaded eight boats per week, amounting to about 320 tons of coal. For this they received 3s.8d. per boat each. In the eighteen-sixties they were described thus to a government committee by Mr. Worsnop:

"Coalheavers are a very improvident class of men, and a very large number of them sel-

Two views showing housing conditions in the area adjoining the canal.

dom have a change of clothes for themselves or families. To give an instance of one who might be considered a decent fellow of the general run. He lives in a cellar at a rental of 2s.3d. per week. He has a wife and four children. They are all clad in rags which are often filthy. The children are so small as to be unable to help themselves, and frequently are left for a day together without food or fire, and if it were not for the kindness of some of the neighbours who are far worse off in the matter of income, these poor children would be found almost starving, whilst both parents are off drinking."[22]

Among the other canal based trades were the night soil men. They collected the town's refuse which was then sent by canal to be used as agricultural fertiliser. Those loading the boats worked in gangs of three and were able to fill about six boats per week for which they received 24 shillings each (3 shillings per boat).

The consequences of living and working in such conditions were not widely realised until 1844, when Dr Duncan, who became Liverpool's first Medical Officer of Health, was examined by the Commissioners inquiring into the state of large towns. His figures showed that Liverpool had the highest death rate in the country. The average age at death was seventeen years, with 1 in 28.75 of the population dying each year. The comparable figures for London were 26.5 years and 1 in 37.38. The worst conditions of all were in the district surrounding the canal basin. Many houses used by the poorest sections of the community were built in enclosed courts, and access was often through a covered passage under one of the houses. This meant that there was inadequate ventilation to the whole court. At the bottom of the heap, many people lived in cellars, and as the underlying soil was clay and adequate drainage was rarely provided, these often became flooded. There were few sewers and the middens provided instead often leaked, so the conditions in such cellars must have been appalling. Besides the problems of sewage, overcrowding was common, with seven or eight people often sharing a single room. Children were sometimes sent to dameschools where little was taught and the overcrowding continued. Mr. Wood described one in the eighteen-thirties as being,

"...in a garret up three pairs of dark, broken stairs, with forty children in the compass of ten feet by nine, and where, on a perch forming a triangle with the corner of the room sat a cock and two hens; under a stump-bed immediately beneath was a dog kennel, in the occupation of three black terriers, whose barking, added to the noise of the children and the cackling of the fowls on the approach of a stranger was almost deafening. There was only one small window, at which sat the master, obstructing three-fourths of the light it was capable of admitting."[23]

Aerial view of Liverpool c.1860 showing the canal basin. Although sailing barges are depicted they never worked on the canal.

The Eye Hospital now occupies these offices, built c1800 for the coal trade. For many years they were used by the Wigan Coal and Iron Company whose boats delivered to Clarke's Basin immediately behind the offices.

With such conditions fever broke out regularly and contagious diseases were endemic. Small wonder that the death rate was so high.

To combat the unhealthy conditions in the area the Northern Hospital had been set up in 1834. It originally occupied a house belonging to R.B. Blundell-Hollinshead at No.1 Leeds Street, where twenty beds were provided. Adjacent houses were taken over in 1836 and 1838, by which time 106 beds were available. These premises were soon insufficient, and in 1843 a purpose built hospital was erected, backing onto the canal basin, next door to the gaol. The old site in Leeds Street became a weighing bridge office for coal brought by canal.[24] However, provision of a hospital did not solve the problem of ill-health. Dr. Duncan, together with Mr. Newlands, the Borough Engineer, set about alleviating the cause by improving the disposal of refuse and night soil in a scheme which was to provide traffic for the canal for many years.

The Manure Traffic

There were three main types of refuse: street sweepings which included dirt and mud from the unmade roads, together with horse manure from the traffic using them; vegetable refuse, ashes and other household rubbish; and finally night soil. The first two were fairly innocuous, and could be collected at any time of day, though the ashes required picking over later to remove any clinker and coal which was then used in burning combustible rubbish. It was the night soil which was the problem. At this time, few sewers had been laid, and even the better class of house would have its own midden. These could leak, the liquor contaminating the immediate neighbourhood, especially any cellars. There was one bonus with the middens that leaked – they did not smell so offensively when they were cleaned out! This was only done on request, so many in the worst areas would not be emptied for months, with inevitable consequences. When the scavenging department was asked to empty a midden this was undertaken after twelve o'clock at night, hence the term night soil. However, many middens were situated in alleys which could only be reached by barrows. The night soil was then deposited on the pavement at the end of the alley for removal by horse drawn cart, often late in the morning. The refuse and night soil were then dumped on canalside wharfs to await sorting and loading before it could finally leave the town.

For many years the main wharf was at Phillips Street where three short arms were built in 1864 for loading boats. Other wharfs were at Burlington Street, Sandhills and at Harrington Dock, though Phillips Street was by far the most important. In the eighteen-sixties it was estimated that over 4,000 tons of refuse were removed weekly, while a further 3,000 tons of night soil were delivered to the canal wharfs.[25] Here it was eventually loaded into boats and taken out to the farms of West Lancashire where it was used as fertiliser. It was certainly fortuitous that the soils there required this type of fertiliser and not the lime which the canal had originally been built to supply.

To cope with such an unpleasant cargo the boats were specially adapted; the planks lining the hold were caulked to make them water-tight and an extra bulkhead was fitted at each end to give an air gap between the cargo and the living accommodation. When they were being loaded it was not uncommon for manure to spill into the canal, while the bilge water pumped out of the boats was described as "as of the foulest description".[26] Samples were analysed and found to be sixty eight times more noxious than normal sewage; small wonder that the canal company did not allow boats to be pumped out in the basin area where there was no flow to purify the water. Surprisingly, Mr. Tatham the canal manager, stated that the 150 tons of mud dredged from the basin each week did not smell, attributing this to a reaction with the other refuse which fell into the water. Coal dust was also thought to purify the water, and considerable quantities must have fallen into the canal from Meyrick Bankes & Co's. coal yard which was opposite the manure wharf. The suggested purification may well have occurred, as later in the century charcoal was added to sewage in house middens and ashpits to reduce the smell. Tatham considered the neighbourhood of the manure wharf to be particularly healthy, though the Medical Officer of Health's mortality figures tell a very different tale. Earlier, in 1853, Tatham had moved from his house alongside the canal near the basin, at which time he had complained that it was unhealthy.[27] Perhaps he was not too worried so long as his own family was not at risk, though, to be charitable, his judgement may have been affected by overwork as he suffered a nervous breakdown in the late eighteen-sixties.

Railway Competition

The opening of the Bolton and Leigh Railway in 1828 and the Liverpool and Manchester in 1830, brought the first real opposition to the canal's trade, causing a reduction in tolls for goods to Wigan, Leigh and Manchester. However, it was not until the East Lancashire, and Lancashire and Yorkshire railways opened to their station in Great Howard Street in 1848 that the canal's income began to suffer. The railway's Great Howard Street station was very inconvenient, as the canal basin effectively blocked access from the town. To overcome this, they proposed to build a new terminus in Tithebarn Street, with their line into the station crossing the canal basin. Since their plan entailed the demolition of the warehouses off Back Leeds Street, used by the Union Company for much of the canal's merchandise traffic, there was considerable opposition. The basin was already overcrowded, and storage space for timber, stone and coal, all important traffics, would also disappear. There were further

Great Howard Street Goods Depot of the L & YR in 1913. The original canal basin was crossed by the lattice girder bridge. The sidings on the right hand side being built on top of the basin. Behind the railway viaduct are the canal company's warehouses built in the eighteen-sixties with the company's office on the extreme right. City Engineers' Department, Liverpool City Council.

worries about fires caused by the locomotives. The canal company wrote complaining:

"It may not be improper to observe that many of the goods which pass along the canal and which are necessarily exposed upon their wharfs continually are highly combustible, such as cotton, flax, oil, spirits, turpentine and even gunpowder, some of which articles railway companies refuse on account of the great danger there is from the sparks of fire which are emitted from their engines continually.

The business which was transmitted last year upon the wharfs proposed to be passed over by the railway was about 100,000 tons cotton, timber and general merchandise, 20,000 tons of flags, stone and bricks, and 8,000 tons of coal, all of which had to be carted either into or out of the town of Liverpool and for which these wharfs are conveniently situated.

The method of carting timber in Liverpool is by the means of wheels of great diameter to which the baulks, sometimes 60 feet long, are slung and dropped upon the timber wharf wherever the carter can find a vacant space and although the wharf is large it is frequently filled."[28]

In spite of the opposition, the extension was approved but it had to pass over the basin on a viaduct, missing the warehouses and thus reducing any interference to the canal's trade.

One result of competition for traffic between the railways and the canal was that merchandise carrying on the canal was leased to the railway companies for twenty-one years from 1851. This caused a reduction in goods carried by the canal, but brought in a guaranteed income.

Following representations from many East Lancashire merchants in the early eighteen-seventies who were unhappy about the service given by the Lancashire and Yorkshire Railway, the company decided to revive merchandise carrying. As a result considerable improvements were carried out all along the canal to facilitate cargo handling. At the basin, new offices and a warehouse were built on Old Hall Street in 1873. The following year a steam crane was installed on the timber quay. This must have been successful, as steam engines, each powering several cranes, were soon fitted in the main warehouses. 1877 saw a large investment, of over £3,000 in a provender store, veterinary services and stabling for the company's horses.[29] It was located at 35 Leeds Street, on the corner with Tinklepeg Lane, and was leased by Joseph Leather and Sons, veterinary surgeons, in 1879. It was soon to be demolished in radical changes to the area.

The Extension of Pall Mall

For many years the Town Council had been concerned about the poor road system to the north of the town. The canal basin effectively blocked the way, and though it was possible to use Old Hall Street, the hump backed bridge over the arm to Clarke's Basin made it difficult for heavily loaded horse-drawn vehicles. To solve the problem they proposed to extend Pall Mall through to Love Lane. At the same time the Lancashire and Yorkshire Railway wanted to enlarge their station in Tithebarn Street. Because the canal had to be crossed, this had been built at a high level so the public had to ascend stairs to the trains. Initially these two schemes were separate, the railway's being proposed in 1876, while the Corporation obtained an Act in 1878 for the new Pall Mall in which the basin was crossed by a bridge. In 1882 all three parties got together and agreement was reached for the canal basin to be filled in to the west of the extended Pall Mall and sufficient land then sold to the railway for their scheme.

*The old hump back bridge in Old Hall Street looking towards the city
centre. It was finally removed in 1902, twenty years after the old basin
had been filled in. This greatly improved access to the north docks from
the city centre. City Engineers Department, Liverpool City Council.*

There were several good reasons for the Canal Company's agreement:
despite modernisation, many of their facilities were old-fashioned; their
finances were always tight; and their household coal trade, much of
which used the western side of the basin, was declining as railways opened small coal yards in the suburbs. The scheme would provide them
with modern warehouses, equal to any the railways owned, while the
land released would give them a regular source of income from rents or
sales. Work was soon in hand and the old terminus finally closed in August 1886. The tenants of the old basin were compensated for the inconvenience and arrangements made for new premises. Wigan Coal and
Iron Company, perhaps the largest coal supplier on the canal, moved
from their yards in Back Leeds Street and Carruthers Street to a new site
on Commercial Road. This was certainly smaller than before and, as
they required no compensation for the loss of a twenty-four stall stable,
suggests that their household coal trade was declining.

*Boatwomen take a moment's rest on a boat moored in the canal basin.
c1900. Authors collection.*

New warehousing was built along Pall Mall and can still be seen,
though that erected in Leeds Street was pulled down recently when the
road was widened. The alterations and new warehouses cost some
£50,000, though the Company received over £100,000 as compensation,
thus making a considerable profit.[30] At the same time a three storey office block was built in Pall Mall by Roberts and Robinson at a cost of
£7,908. Beside the usual board rooms and toll office needed by a canal,
there was an engineering drawing office and a freight office for the
Company's fleet of boats. These offices were destroyed by bombing during the Second World War, though fortunately many of the Company's
legal records had been moved to a strong room built at Bank Newton
maintenance yard near Gargrave, while the traffic office had been
removed to Blackburn.

The moral welfare of canal workers in Liverpool was not neglected
when the Liverpool and Wigan Canal Mission was established by Mr.
and Mrs. Wood in 1864. Financial support was received from the Canal
Company, who also provided premises at the basin. There certainly
seems to have been an improvement in conditions, Moses Jackson of the

Mission complaining in 1876 to the Secretary of State about George Smith's tirade on the poor conditions endured by boatmen:[31]

> "This I am bound to deny and am assured by all the residents near the canal between Liverpool and Wigan that within the last twelve years the transformation which had taken place in the boatpeople is really wonderful in cleanliness, language and general conduct."[32]

He went on to say that 50% could read, only 20% could be classed as drunkards, and not more than 1% were living as man and wife unmarried. Most had homes on the bank and at least 50% of the children went to school. Much of the change in attitude had resulted from the influence of the Mission. From 1878 the Mission moved to the old canal offices and, in 1891, they amalgamated with the Mersey Mission to Seamen. New premises on Pall Mall were built in 1908 and were extended the following year, at the boatmen's suggestion, by the provision of a small shooting gallery. Obviously many boatmen wanted to keep their poaching skills sharp whilst in town! The Mission closed in the mid thirties. It has since been demolished but part of the frontage on Pall Mall remains.

"and the place thereof shall know it no more"; all that remains of the Boatmen's Mission.

More Manure

The manure and refuse traffic continued to thrive as the population grew. The construction of sewers was progressing and consequently night soil was becoming less important as a cargo. However, this was more than offset by the increase in household refuse. Carr Hall farm, near Burscough, had been purchased by the Corporation in 1871, and 90,000 tons of refuse was dumped there over the following three years. Local farmers complained and the dumping ceased, the Corporation instead paying canalside farmers about 9d per ton for permission to discharge refuse unsuitable for manure on their lands. This class of refuse was the most difficult to dispose of,[33] so in the early eighteen-eighties two steam hopper barges, *Alpha* and *Beta*, were purchased to take the refuse out into Liverpool bay where it was dumped beyond the Bar. *Alpha* worked from the South Docks while the *Beta*, which could carry 400 tons, was loaded in Collingwood Dock by hand from canal barges. This was found to be very slow, so to improve matters new iron canal barges were built to carry twenty-four steel framed wooden boxes, each box taking about 2 tons of refuse. These were loaded at the canalside refuse depots and then delivered to the docks where they were emptied into the hopper barge. It took twenty minutes to unload each canal barge using this system, which employed just four men instead of the thirty odd needed previously.[34]

Better ways of disposing of rubbish were continually being sought, and in 1891 a twelve cell destructor was installed at the Charters Street Wharf. Two years later it was enlarged by a further twelve cells. In these cells the refuse was burnt, its weight being reduced by two thirds, and the resulting ash and clinker used to make paving slabs and mortar. Electricity was also generated and used to light the surrounding area, whilst the waste steam was used to disinfect contaminated clothing.[35]

The manure traffic to canalside farms was to continue well into the nineteen-forties, only declining as more and more houses were connected to the sewerage system. In the eighteen-sixties there were complaints about manure remaining on the wharf in Liverpool and creating a health hazard. To overcome this the Corporation purchased manure wharfs in West Lancashire, subsequently insisting manure should be loaded directly into boats in Liverpool and only stored on those wharfs' outside the town. In theory the manure was only allowed to remain for

Charters Street destructor in 1906. The boats include both those deliver-
ing containers of rubbish for transshipment in Waterloo Dock and the
canal barges which took refuse to West Lancashire for use as fertilizer.
City Engineer's Department, Liverpool City Council.

seven days maximum at these country wharfs but this was often disregarded. The tonnages carried were immense with over 7,000 tons being delivered to one wharf in Lydiate in six months. Well over 100,000 tons were removed from Liverpool annually. The boatmen were paid on the tonnage carried and in 1904 the Lancashire Farmers Union at Ormskirk complained that dry manure was dampened with canal water by the boatmen to increase the weight, sometimes by 10 or 15 tons.[36] The added water could have made the manure considerably more offensive and Mr. Tomlinson, a Burscough J.P., complained in 1884 about the state of the local manure wharfs:

"It is monstrous that such accumulations should be tolerated in the midst of such a populous village. Honest horse and cow manure deserves respect, but the villainous compounds that are positively ennobled by being styled manure reek with noxious odours that send one home to Sunday dinner many a time with a sickened appetite."[37]

The manure certainly had a bad reputation, though this was well deserved by all accounts. The boatmen involved in its carriage did not usually complain of the smell, but those on other boats always tried to keep out of their way and loathed having to follow one of the manure boats.

Electric Power

1897 saw the purchase, by the Corporation, of the Liverpool Tramway Company. It was decided to electrify the system and one of the two power stations built for the system was at Pumpfields, adjacent to the canal. Twelve Willans vertical triple expansion engines were installed producing 15,000 hp, generating electricity at 460-500 volts dc.[38] This was used for street lighting as well as for the trams. Coal, brought by boat, was unloaded onto a conveyor that led to the boiler house. The canalside site had the added advantage that the canal could be used for cooling the condensers, though this waste heat was to have an adverse effect as we shall see later.

The Twentieth Century

Following the First World War, during which government policy had

Pumpfields Power Station in the early stages of demolition 1991.

seriously damaged the profitability of canals, the Leeds and Liverpool decided to give up its carrying fleet. From 1921 this was sold piecemeal to various by-traders. They also gave up their warehouses, those in Liverpool eventually being sold to the Mersey Wharfage Company in 1927, though preferential treatment there was ensured for canal carriers. In 1936, by which time they had become the Liverpool Warehousing Company Ltd, they were complaining about the temperature of the canal. Tate and Lyle had installed new plant which relied upon the canal for condensing water, and this, together with the Corporation electricity works was raising the temperature of the water excessively. In November they wrote:

"During the last couple of days visibility in the yards has been nil, causing loading operations by crane and warehouse hoist to be dangerous.

Men certainly cannot work under prevailing conditions without serious risk to their health, one man is, in fact, absent from duty with chest trouble, certainly aggravated by the continuous damp conditions...

Chisenhale Street bridge in 1935 showing the problem of overheating. The 'Liddisdale' on the left was one of Abel's dumb flats built for use in the docks along the canal in Liverpool. City Engineers Department, Liverpool City Council.

Goods in store are of course badly affected, and although we have succeeded in disposing of parcels of cattle cake damaged by surface mould, I am nervous that a time will come when this contamination will be noticed."[39]

The Canal Company complained to Tate and Lyle's who subsequently erected cooling towers to remove most of the heat before water was let back into the canal.

The Second World War caused considerable interference to the canal. The Liverpool section was closed for six months following major bomb damage at Sandhills. The Head Office was also destroyed by bombing, though the warehouses survived. As in the First World War, government was loath to provide canals with the financial help received by railways, and this, combined with the demise of traditional canalside industry, brought about the final decline of canal carrying. Boats had ceased to use the basin for several years when, in 1960, it was filled in as part of the redevelopment of Tate and Lyle's site, bringing to an end almost two hundred years of canal transport in central Liverpool.

Leeds & Liverpool Canal Company's office c1960. It had been destroyed by bombing during the Second World War. J. Parkinson.

The Basin Area Today

Today there is a surprising amount left, considering the recent wholesale changes to the city centre. From before the eighteen-eighties reorganisation, only the former coal office remains in Old Hall Street, though the canal bridge here remained for twenty years after the basin was closed, being used as a cellar for the adjacent buildings. Clarke's Basin disappeared when King Edward Street was built across the site in 1904. Thomas Bennett & Co's cooperage expanded into the area from their original premises in Brook Street, but these too have now disappeared together with the warehouses in Bath Street which were pulled down about fifteen years ago.

In Pall Mall all the warehousing remains, together with the foreman's house, while a modern office occupies the space left when the canal's offices were destroyed. Towards Chisenhale Street can be seen the frontage of the Boatmen's Mission, built on the site of the old toll office. In Chisenhale Street itself the canal bridge remains alongside the former Bridge pub, now a decorators. Less is left in Leeds Street, where all the warehouses have been demolished, but this does make finding the basin site, still surrounded by coping stones, simple. In the streets that surrounded the arms off the main basin can be found many old buildings, though few were directly connected with the canal. The only large building remaining is the Pumpfields Electricity Station,[40] easily seen from Vauxhall Road, which backed onto the canal.

3
Down to the River

Liverpool in the eighteenth century was fast developing into the main English port for trade with the American colonies. The woollen merchants of Bradford saw great opportunities in these markets, and the Leeds and Liverpool Canal, it was hoped, was one way of improving access for their goods to colonial shipping there. One advantage canal traffic has over other forms of transport is that canal boats can transfer cargoes to and from seagoing vessels directly, without the use of wharfs or quays. To capitalise on this a clause was inserted in the canal's first Act authorising a branch linking the canal to the river, thus enabling such transhipment to take place. Unfortunately Liverpool's Town Council, through their lease and subsequent purchase of the township lands from Lord Molyneux in 1671, controlled the foreshore. They also owned the dock system, allowing them to restrict the opportunities open to the canal for a branch to the river or for a connection to the docks. Proposals for such a link surfaced regularly in the years following the passing of the canal's first Act in 1770, but it was not until 1846 that it was finally constructed.

Until the eighteenth century local government and industry had been dominated by the interests of titled land owners, but both Liverpool and the Leeds and Liverpool Canal were precursors of a new age where decisions would be made by merchants rather than landed gentry. Until the mid-nineteenth century, when Parliament began to take more interest in local government and the co-ordination of industry and transport, this resulted in parochial attitudes. These were much in evidence in the dealings between the fiercely independent merchants of Lancashire and Yorkshire, and were to delay the construction of a link between the canal and the docks.

A Link to the River

The Town Council had supported the initial promotion and surveys for the canal but when the canal's Act was being sought they ensured that a clause asserted that only they could construct a branch to the dock system and that a link to the river, separate from the docks, was all that could be built by the canal. This attitude of the Council was to prevail for the next seventy years, despite the problems it would cause, and as a result, the canal had to change the site of its scheme for a branch to the river repeatedly, to avoid new docks as they extended northwards.

After the 1770 Act had been obtained, work in Lancashire was concentrated on constructing the canal from Liverpool to the Douglas Navigation so that coal could be supplied to the town from Wigan. The committee decided to hold the river link in abeyance until after the opening of that section of canal.[41] By mid-1774 it was open. As it had cost far more than expected, though, a waggonway was suggested to link the docks to the canal basin; this was cheaper to construct. There was still the possibility of a branch, but the Town Council warned that the 1770 Act did not allow this to join their new dock,[42] and that the line should be moved further north so as not to interfere with dock extensions.

A year passed with no solution to the problem, though Mr. Eagle, the canal's solicitor, was asked by the committee if their Act gave authority for the construction of the waggonway. The Company's problems were increased when the War Office decided at the end of 1775 to build their new barracks and fort for the protection of the port on the very piece of land earmarked for the branch. Despite these setbacks, arrangements went ahead for the branch, coal yards being located on the eastern side of the canal basin so as not to interfere with construction. A committee was appointed to confer with the Town Council in the hope of financial assistance for the scheme, but there must still have been considerable local ill-feeling against those controlling the canal in Yorkshire. The Liverpool men must have decided to get their own back for the Yorkshire proprietors' intransigence over the canal route through Lancashire, and insisted on the letter of the Act which required the Company to pay for the construction of the branch.[43]

At the beginning of 1776 the Town Council then complained that the line proposed interfered with their new dock works and asked for it to be moved 100 yards to the north. Henry Berry, their Dock Engineer, would then check this line and produce a plan agreeable to the Council. They also insisted that a bridge be built on the road along the shore where it would be crossed by the canal. By April the Canal Company, whose finances were virtually exhausted, again asked for financial assistance in building the branch. This the Council refused, reminding the canal that they must make all the works at their own expense. They also disagreed with the new scheme, though seemed adverse to explaining why. The Canal Company then replied demanding recompense for having to alter their Parliamentary line. The two sides must have agreed to postpone building the branch, but we shall never know definitely as the Canal Company minutes are missing for the following month.[44] Relations soon improved as eighteen months later Henry Berry was allowed to use the clay originally purchased by the Canal for the branch for a road to the new fort. It was considered superfluous as the existing links to the docks, by horse drawn waggon, were to be continued.

A Coal Dock is Planned

Merchandise had been the main reason behind the initial proposal for a dock branch, but when three plans were presented to the committee, in 1787, for a canal into the Mersey, it was the export of coal which was foremost in the promoters' minds. The idea of making Liverpool into a major coal exporter was resurrected several times in the following sixty years. On this occasion it was probably brought about by the decision of Lord Balcarres, the main Wigan coalowner, to develop the export of his coal and cannel to Paris.[45] There was some success, but not enough to warrant a new dock and branch.

1802 saw the next attempt, Fletcher, the canal's engineer, setting out a line to the proposed new north docks. The Council were approached as their consent was needed, but no further action taken. The Act for Princes Dock had been passed three years earlier, and the branch would have joined this new dock. However, its construction was postponed, the southern docks being developed instead, and it was not until 1821 that Princes Dock was opened, the suspension of work on the northern docks adversely affecting the canal. A Bill for the improvement of the southern docks was presented in 1811, when the canal company petitioned against it, stating that Princes Dock should be built first. They were concerned that goods interchanged between the canal and the docks, transported by horse drawn waggons, had to cross the town to reach the southern docks. This was a much longer and more expensive journey than to the northern docks. Mr. Hustler, one of the Wigan colliery owners wrote to the company complaining:

"The principal part of our sale is with Ireland considerable to America, and the coasting vessels to Wales etc, at present vessels so employed find births in the three west docks,

Repairs to the bottom lock in October 1954. Note the masonry, typical of Jesse Hartley's work in the docks. The Lune in the background was built for carrying general cargo on the canal in the nineteen-thirties. Authors collection.

viz. Georges Dock, the Old Dock, and Salthouse Dock, and for *coasters*, the bason near the fort; and the cartage to those places is very reasonable say from 1/- to 1/6 per ton."[46]

He goes on to say that any increase in costs will make coal from Prescot and the Sankey Navigation more attractive to purchasers to the detriment of the canal's trade. Princes Dock, adjacent to the canal basin, would materially reduce the congestion and expense caused by such traffic. A compromise was eventually reached in which the time for completion of the dock works, both north and south, was agreed, though there were still doubts as to the availability of berths in the south docks for small coasting vessels in the coal trade.

Two years later the Canal Company proposed to build a dock and basin, to be called Regents and Derby Docks respectively, for these vessels, on land to the north of the unfinished Princes Dock. The scheme was drawn up by William Chapman, a London engineer, who surveyed four lines between the canal and the river, two from the basin and two from the canal.[47] He preferred one from near the basin which would descend four locks into a dock 270 feet by 110 feet which could accomodate six of the vessels then used in the coastal coal trade. Coal yards would line one side of the basin which it was hoped would handle 120,000 tons annually. However, the Dock Committee asked too high a price for the land required and the plan was shelved. The scheme for a branch was not abandoned, and in 1825 the Company had a clause inserted in a new dock Bill which allowed them to move its position to the north.

The Branch is Built

In 1834 there was an abortive proposal for a branch into the recently opened Clarence Dock,[48] but it was not until 1844 and the Act for Stanley Dock, that concrete proposals for a dock branch were agreed. It was to be built by the Dock Committee who would then sell it to the Canal Company for £50,000. In the event, some of the land between Great Howard Street and Regent Road was retained by the Dock Committee reducing the price to £42,622. Several schemes were drawn up by Jesse

Transshipping containers of refuse from boats loaded on the canal into the Beta for dumping in Liverpool Bay. Note the lifting bridge on the Overhead Railway which allowed access for ships into Stanley Dock. Liverpool Library.

Hartley, the Dock Engineer. In one, Stanley Dock was omitted, the canal entering directly into Collingwood Dock, whilst another had a dock from the eastern end of Stanley Dock parallel to, and to the south of the branch. This was resurrected in 1857 and again in 1872, though nothing came of the it. The Canal Company provided outline plans for the locks but they were built by Jesse Hartley, the Dock Engineer, to his own design and show masonary typical of his work on the rest of the dock estate.

A lockhouse was built by the Canal Company at the top of the locks, and men were employed round the clock, Monday to Saturday, by the Dock Committee, to control the movement of boats to and from the docks. There was a toll on goods which had not paid Dock Dues, and the certificates giving the load carried by each barge from which this was calculated were collected by these men. The locks could be used on Sundays, though prior arrangements had to be made with the Dock Committee. Coal was the main traffic, and in 1851, three years after the branch had opened, 303 boats delivered coal from Wigan to the docks, 134 took coal from Wigan to Cheshire, seven carried wheat from George's Dock to Blackburn, six carried timber from Toxteth Dock to Accrington and four carried flags from Burnley to Birkenhead. There

Entrance to Stanley Dock in 1990. Author's Collection.

were many more small cargoes besides.[49] The collection of tolls ceased from 2nd December 1960 as there was insufficient traffic then to make it worth while.

Traffic to and from the docks developed rapidly, and more branches were suggested, although none were ever completed. In 1850 the old plan to link the basin with Princes Dock re-emerged, then four years later the Dock Committee proposed a branch canal into a new dock they were planning. This was one of the early schemes for Canada Dock in which six small docks and two large timber docks were to be built, the latter on reclaimed land. There were also to be five graving docks. This dock system was to be connected to the main canal by four locks, possibly built as a single four-rise lock, on a branch parallel to Castle Street in Bootle.[50] The Canal Company insisted on a six mile minimum toll and were concerned to limit the depth of the locks to 11 feet to reduce the water usage.

Improved connections with the docks were suggested on two further occasions, in 1864 and in 1884. On the former occasion it was thought that a new wharf at Sandhills would serve just as well. Warde-Aldam,

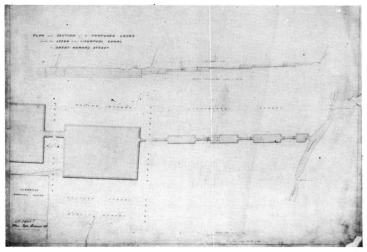

The locks at Stanley Dock were built by the Dock Committee, hence this drawing came from Jesse Hartley's office. It is not signed by him because it was not the "as built" version.

one of the directors wrote of the wharf:

"It is very favourably situated for cartage traffic to the docks. The vessels going down the locks only communicate with 2 or 3 docks, but this wharf communicates, within a very short distance, by Sandhills Lane into the Regent Road, which runs along the line of docks. Whether for coal, timber or stone it is very convenient for traffic with the docks."[51]

One of the problems with canal access to the docks was that they did not all interconnect at that time. To pass along the line several tidal basins had to be crossed which made the trip time consuming. This was why wharfs on the canal were a better means of communication, and why the increased costs of transshipment were offset by speed of delivery. Later the tidal basins were removed, dramatically improving the access for canal boats and removing the need for new branches.

There was one more attempt to build a second link to the docks. In the eighteen-nineties plans were drawn up for a branch running parallel to Balliol Road down to Brocklebank Dock.[52] There were to be two sets of two rise locks, with space for boats to pass between. It was hoped that the scheme would reduce the time taken for canal boats to reach the

A view down Liverpool Locks 1973. Note the old wool warehouse in the background. Philip Watkinson.

most northerly docks, but there was probably insufficient traffic to make the expense worthwhile.

Around the Branch

There had been little development of the Lightbody Street area prior to the construction of the branch. The land to the south was owned by the Dock Committee, and workshops used for the maintenance and construction of docks were built here shortly after the branch opened. These became less important as the docks progressed northward and in 1895 they were replaced by a large wool warehouse. Wool for delivery to Yorkshire was a major traffic on the canal, and the Company suggested that an arm should be built from the branch into the new warehouse. The Dock Board would not entertain this and instead raised gangways were suggested to enable bales to be carried over the towpath and then lowered into boats underneath.

A variety of flats and barges in the south docks. A large packing case is being transhipped from a Leeds & Liverpool barge. It probably contains textile machinery made in east Lancashire which was a major traffic on the canal.

A branch was built for the Bridgewater Canal above the first lock in 1856. The Bridgewater's depots were all in the south docks and this basin and warehouse were to serve vessels in the more recent northern docks. Canal companies usually had problems co-operating especially, as here, where they were in competition. There were arguments about the tolls charged for the use of the few yards of canal necessary to reach the Bridgewater's warehouse, the two companies ending up in court before a compromise was reached. The depot proved expensive for the Bridgewater and they had vacated the premises by 1910.

Between the canal and Lightbody Street were several small yards. During the nineteenth century most were occupied by slate merchants, many Lancashire roofs being covered with Welsh slate carried by canal from Liverpool. By the end of the century this traffic had been taken by the railways who could deliver without the need to transship, thus reducing breakage. In their place were coal yards, the chemical works of G. Hadfield & Co., and the Anglo American Oil Co. stores. Hadfield's remained there for many years producing artificial fertiliser. The oil stores were expanded during the twentieth century and Shell Mex and B.P. also had premises here by the nineteen-thirties. The Dock Board built a canalside refuse destructor at 38 Lightbody Street where rubbish from the docks was burnt. It is still operated by the Bootle Barge Company.

4
Industry and the Canal

Liverpool in the second half of the eighteenth century was one of the major manufacturing centres of Lancashire, and it was the need for a supply of coal to industry that was the main reason behind the promotion of the canal in the town. Compared to the rest of Lancashire the local merchants were well established and considered themselves more refined, the phrase "Manchester men, Liverpool gentlemen" reflecting this view. They were less inclined to have their environment polluted by industry and, for this reason, had already forced a copper refinery to leave the town. This attitude, together with the rise in land values and increase in wages, brought about by the success of the port, resulted in a decline in the importance of manufacturing industry in the town and the rise of service industries such as food processing and packaging.

Originally industry tended to be located near to the docks. There were some canalside factories built in the years after the canal opened, but it was not until the rapid development of the northern dock system in the mid-nineteenth century that there was significant growth in their number. It is possible the canal and its terminal basin may well have had some bearing on the initially slow extension of the docks northward because they created a barrier to the easy movement of road traffic between the town centre and the northern foreshore. Certainly the humpback bridge over the canal in Old Hall Street was a continual source of traffic congestion until it was removed early in the twentieth century. A further bar to Liverpool's development northward was the independence of the township of Bootle. It was not until late in the nineteenth century that Liverpool finally realised that it was unlikely to incorporate Bootle within its boundaries. Only after this was there growth of housing, industry and services between them.

The nineteenth century saw great changes on the canal banks. Agriculture declined steadily, being replaced by housing and industry. Even the location of these altered over the years. Because of the complexity of the development along the canal corridor we will look at which industries were in operation there at the beginning, in the middle, and at the end of the nineteenth century. The rise and fall of the Liverpool chemical industry took place during this period, and there were many canal-side sites.

The primary role of the canal during its first fifty years of operation in Lancashire was to supply Liverpool with coal. This was delivered to an ever increasing number of coal wharfs around the basin from where it was transported by road to factories and docks. Several industries soon transferred to sites alongside the canal where coal could be supplied directly. Soap, glass and chemical factories were especially keen to move to such sites in the undeveloped northern part of the town where their pollution would be less problematical.

All three industries were based on alkali.[53]This was imported in the naturally occurring forms of barilla, kelp or potash, from which it was then extracted. Soap making was, perhaps, the most important of the three industries, Liverpool rivalling the traditional production centre of London by the nineteenth century. The town's soft soap industry, which used vegetable oils imported from the colonies, soon came to dominate the market. The process created much waste soda which was then used in glass bottle making. Besides soap and glass manufacture, alkali was increasingly used during the processing of textiles, with vitriol (sulphuric acid) and bleaching powder (from chlorine) being produced at canalside factories. Pollution from reactions using these chemicals, as we shall see later, became a major disincentive to the development of the industry in a heavily populated town. The chemical industry developed because the rapid increase in the demand for alkali by the soap, glass and textile industries required a synthetic product, that available naturally proving inadequate. Besides coal delivered by the canal, the ease of supply of salt from Cheshire was an important factor in the decision to locate the industry in Liverpool, salt being one of the basic raw materials for the production of synthetic alkali.

The Canal in 1800

In 1800 the canal approached Liverpool through agricultural lands, with only the occasional factory. The first to be noticed was just before the bridge at Stanley Road in Bootle, then known as Stamp House Swing Bridge,[54] where the Bootle Glass House could be seen across a field to the south. Bootle springs, from where water had been piped to supply Liverpool for just a year, could also be seen across the fields. After passing through Stamp House Bridge there was a tan house for curing leather on the left, but the surroundings were still predominantly agricultural. Before the next bridge the Bootle Coffee House[55] could be seen to the north, beyond the dam and lodge which supplied water to the waterwheel at Bootle Mills where there was also a windmill. Just before leaving Bootle there was a potash house between the canal and the fore shore, used to the supply the soap industry which was developing around Liverpool.

The canal continued through farming land, passed Bank Hall and Vaux Hall, the next industrial site being Messrs. Moore and Gouthwaite's glass bottle works. This was located at Gerard Bridge, almost opposite where the dock branch was built forty-six years later. Next to the works was a windmill for grinding corn, operated by the Halewood

Old boilers are often used for storage of liquids as here at the old Litherland Tannery.

family. There were many windmills in Liverpool at this time. The milling industry was to be a major user of the canal throughout its working life.

The canal now passed through open land until Chisenhale Street Bridge where Mr. Porter had recently opened his lead works. After the bridge the terminal basin was reached. The Bootle Waterworks Company's yard and reservoir between the canal and Vauxhall Road was fed by a pipeline from Bootle springs. A steam pumping engine was used to supply the town, the area becoming known as Pumpfields. Other steam engines were already established in the area, Bateman, Greaves & Co. having been allowed to use the canal water for their engine from 1791. There were other industries, such as soap and chemical works, round the basin, while a cotton mill, known as Union Mill, was being operated by Messrs. Kirkman & Co. on the east side of Vauxhall Road.[56] This was unsuccessful and was later taken over by Messrs. G. Forrester & Co. for use as a foundry.

Developments by 1850

In 1800 Georges Dock was the furthest north the dock system reached. By 1850 eleven more docks had been built and work was progressing northwards on Sandon and Huskisson Docks. The Lancashire and Yorkshire, and East Lancashire Railways had also entered the town by a route almost parallel to the canal. Much of this development had occurred over the preceding ten years and was to radically change the canal corridor as industry and housing followed. Gas lighting, introduced to Liverpool in 1815, was also to provide further traffic to the canal as works were erected alongside.

Industry now reached as far out as Litherland where a tannery had been built five and a half miles from the basin. A second tannery in Litherland, Ashburner's, reflects the importance of the dairy industry in the locality. In the days before refrigeration, milk had to be delivered quickly and most towns had a thriving dairying community on its outskirts. As early as 1775 the canal company had complained about cattle grazing on the tow-path, such trespassers being impounded in West Derby pinfold.[57] Litherland also boasted an asphalt factory and two sandstone quarries, all of which used the canal.

Bootle Glass Works had now been converted to chemical manufacture and had moved to a site right alongside the canal at Bootle bridge. The water works was still operating, but seems to have been the only other industry in the area, though much residential development had taken place between Coffee House Bridge and Bank Hall. The northward progress of the docks had not yet reached Bootle where many Liverpool merchants lived in houses overlooking the estuary. The prevailing westerly winds made this a much pleasanter place than Everton to the east, which suffered from wind-blown industrial pollution from the canalside chemical works nearer to the town.

At Bankhall were the Lancashire and Yorkshire Railway locomotive sheds, water for the engines being taken, by agreement, from the canal.[58]

Athol Street gas works was once a busy place as the numerous loading and unloading doorways show. Several are surrounded by cast iron frames. In the background is the chimney of Bootle Barge Company's refuse destructor.

A siding alongside the canal also allowed goods to be transshipped, though it is uncertain how often this was used. After passing under the railway there was a tile works, the underlying clay to the north of the town being ideal for brick and tile manufacture. The kilns were fired with coal brought by boat from Wigan.

No more development had occurred until Boundary Street, marking the division between Liverpool and Kirkdale, was reached. Here the North Shore Cotton Mills had been erected around 1840. As with other Liverpool textile concerns it only survived for a few years. After standing empty for a short while it was converted into the North Shore Flour and Rice Mills and was the first of several large modern steam powered flour mills to be built alongside the canal.[59]

At the next bridge, Athol Street, was the Liverpool New Gas and Coke Company's works, opened in 1834.[60] This company had originally been set up as the Oil Gas Company in 1823, producing gas from whale oil. Later other oils, such as palm, linseed and herring, were tried in an attempt to reduce costs. Gas produced from oil was more expensive than that from coal. Costs had to be reduced as they were in competition with the Liverpool Gas Light Company, set up in 1815 to supply gas from coal and which had been operating from canalside works at Eccles Street, near Burlington Street since 1829. The Athol Street works allowed the New Company to compete with the Old until 1848 when the two merged to form the Liverpool United Gas Company. The Eccles Street works closed in 1934 while production at Athol Street continued until conversion to natural gas.

Although their product was called coal gas it was generally produced from cannel.[61] Much of this came from the Wigan Coal and Iron Company's pits at Haigh, though later their pits at Crooke and Maypole were the suppliers. In 1849 approximately 30,000 tons were delivered to Athol Street. Four years later a severe winter caused problems in delivery when the canal froze. Instead the cannel was sent to Sandhills by rail where it was transhipped into barges for final delivery. Although the coal company did not have a legal claim for the recovery of their losses, the gas company paid the following bill for their additional expenses:

	£	s	d
Additional cost of conveying 1945 tons of Cannel from Haigh to Sandhills Bridge per Railway	97	5	0
Additional cost of Hauling of Boats of Cannel from Haigh to Melling with extra horses and men	47	17	3
Hauling the said boats thence to Gas Works and boating 1945 tons from Sandhills	111	9	10
Estimated damage done to boats	180	0	0
Loss of horse drowned	50	0	0
479 tons of large cannel sent in lieu of small to gain time @ 2/-	47	18	0
	534	10	1

The demand for gas, mainly used for lighting at this time, was at its highest during the cold, short days of winter, and large quantities of cannel were needed. It was vital to keep the canal open if at all possible, though disruption of traffic because of frost was to remain a serious problem for the canal company. In Liverpool this was alleviated because the canal was used as a source of cooling water by canalside industries, resulting in this section rarely being troubled by ice in the late nineteenth and early twentieth century. However, by the nineteen-sixties the decline of canalside industry had reduced the need for cooling water and during the hard winter of 1963/4 the canal froze for many weeks. Because of this canal traffic ceased and the carriage of coal to the gas works was transferred to the railways. It did not last long, as the introduction of natural gas resulted in the closure of the gas works.

The land between the canal and Vauxhall Road was slowly being taken over by a variety of industries. Opposite the gas works were four which were typical. R.P. Gardner & Co. operated a seed crushing plant probably supplying the growing demand for animal feed-stuff. Nearby was Kerr & Mather's steam saw mill, timber being a major Liverpool import with considerable quantities passing along the canal. The sugar industry, long established in Liverpool, was represented by Crosfield, Barrow & Co.'s refinery, while both Fredrick Wedekind and J.T. & A. Fairrie had refineries further along Vauxhall Road. In 1850 Henry Tate was still a retail grocer with five shops,[62] one of which, in Old Hall Street, was near to the canal basin. In 1859 he became a partner in the firm of John Wright and Co., sugar refiners, in Manesty Lane, and it was not until 1870 that he built his innovative refinery in Love Lane, near to the canal. The last of the four representative industries was John Blanchard's flour mill, the grain and flour trade beside the canal being long established.

Muspratt's Chemical Works

Along Vauxhall Road, opposite the flight of locks down to the docks, were several coal wharfs, mainly supplying the domestic market. Beyond these was the extensive chemical works of James Muspratt & Son. This site had originally been occupied by the glass works of Gouthwaite and Moore. James Muspratt,[63] a chemist from Dublin, arrived in Liverpool in 1822, setting up as a potash and vitriol producer on this site the following year. He was soon making soda ash by the Leblanc method in which salt reacts with vitriol to produce alkali (sodium carbonate). Although not the first to utilise this process, the lead lined tanks he constructed to hold the acid were, at 112 feet long by 24 feet wide, many times larger than any in use at that time.

Initially the manufacture of synthetic alkali was little understood which resulted in considerable pollution. The sulphide waste produced was originally dumped near the works, but later was taken away by boat. Methods were eventually discovered for reclaiming much of this sulphur. More of a problem was the muriatic (or hydrochloric) acid gas produced by the reaction of salt with vitriol. The initial solution was to build high towers to allow the gas to be carried away the wind. There were two at Muspratt's works, one of them 250 feet high built in 1835. Unfortunately these just seemed to spread the pollution further, Muspratt being prosecuted more than once for creating a public nuisance.

One case came to court in 1838 in which it was claimed that the gas killed plants and trees, tarnished brass and changed the colour of dyed cloth. The health of those living locally, particularly in Scotland Road and Everton, was also adversely affected. There was a suggestion by some friends of Muspratt that the gas improved health, the prosecution replying facetiously:

> "But it will be said ... that this is a most kindly gas, this muriatic acid gas, that it is exceedingly beneficial, and that, were it not for Mr. Muspratt and his fellow alkali manufacturers, the town of Liverpool would be poisoned."

The notorious chimney of Muspratt's alkali works.

The prosecution then called forty nine witnesses to testify to the damage brought about by the gas. Despite a spirited defence, Muspratt was found guilty and fined, though the works continued in production. It would have been virtually useless to close just one factory in the hope of improvement as at that time there were twelve chemical works, twenty-three distilleries, seventeen soaperies, sixteen breweries, seven lime works, seventeen foundries, two gas works, three sugar houses, three colour factories, five waterworks, and thirteen steam mills, tan yards, and mortar mills in the area surrounding Muspratt's. The abatement of one source of pollution, even though it was a serious one, would have had little beneficial effect on the immediate environment.

James Muspratt originally found it difficult to sell the "black ash" produced by the Leblanc process as the local soap manufacturers seem to have been reluctant to replace natural potash with his synthetic article. It has been suggested that he had not only to give it away but also to supervise its use in soap-making. However, this reluctance was soon overcome and the works continued in production until his death in 1886. By this time he also had factories in Widnes and Flint, his son Edmund becoming the president of the United Alkali Company on its formation in 1890. The Liverpool site, which included eighteen cottages and a shop, was sold to the Canal Company in 1887.

There were three more factories between Muspratt's and Burlington Street Bridge, the distillery of Archibald Walker and two sugar refineries, first Wedekind's then Fairrie's. Through the bridge was Vauxhall Gasworks, while on the other bank was the rice mill of Carstairs & Co. with the Clarence foundry behind. Tenements begin to make their appearance, a large block having been erected by the Council between Chisenhale and Charters Streets. These were an improvement on the poor quality housing to be found elsewhere in the Vauxhall Ward.

At the basin, besides the coal and manure wharfs, were several more chemical and soap works. Of particular note were William Hill on Vauxhall Road and Thomas Lutwyche on Pumpfields,[64] both of whom had been producing synthetic alkali before James Muspratt, though on a small scale. Another well known chemical manufacturer, Charles Kurtz & Son, had premises on Carruthers Street, while Thomas Hadfield's chemical works were on Pumpfields. Besides these chemists there were soap manufacturers, oil merchants, boiler makers, flour millers and a host of smaller businesses clustered round the canal basin. Many operated day and night, and with the continual passage of coal wagons and manure carts the area must have been a hive of activity.

The Twentieth Century

By the turn of the century the dock system was virtually complete. Only two more docks were to be opened, Gladstone in 1927 and Royal Seaforth in 1972. Urbanisation had continued apace, and there was now no interruption to the houses and factories lining the canal between Liverpool and Bootle, while the nearest green fields were as far out as Linacre. This development, together with an acceleration in the pace of life, had lead to considerable increases in road traffic. There were many complaints about the humpback bridges over the canal which were causing problems for the heavily laden horse drawn waggons passing to and

Bankhall Street Warehouse: the last one left on the remainder length which has a shipping hole to allow boats to enter.

from the docks. These bridges were the property of the Canal Company who were not interested in their improvement. It would be costly, and money needed to be spent helping traffic on the canal rather than the road. Instead the local authorities in Liverpool and Bootle agreed to finance bridge reconstruction, taking over the expense of maintenance. Consequently most of the bridges in the area were lowered, enlarged and their carrying capacity increased in the years around 1900.

Where the Canal Company did invest was in the provision of improved warehousing. As has been mentioned above, the basin area was totally rebuilt in the eighteen-nineties when Pall Mall was lengthened, new offices and warehousing being provided at the same time. Previously a new warehouse had been erected in 1874 at Bankhall,[65] boats entering this via a short arm so that they could be loaded under cover. The cranes used for lifting goods here were operated by a small steam engine located next door. It was built by R. & J. Rankin & Co. with a 9 inch diameter piston and 16 inch stroke operating at 60lbs per square inch with steam from a Lancashire boiler 14 feet long by 4 feet 6 inches in diameter. By 1891 this had been replaced by hydraulic power. Further warehousing, costing over £18,000 and opened in 1885, was provided at Carolina Street in Bootle. This became the centre of a small canal community, several boatmen living in the streets nearby. Extensions to the warehouses continued into the twentieth century.

Because of the congestion in town centres, industry was beginning to think about moving to more rural sites. In 1920 it was proposed to build a National Aircraft Factory between the Old Roan and the race-course but the decline in post war armament production removed the need.[66] Not long after, Liverpool Corporation Electricity Department suggested that they would build a power station at Aintree, but this also came to nothing. Twenty years earlier, industrial development still only reached as far out as the canalside tannery at Litherland. The asphalt factory had closed and, possibly as a result, there had been an increase in housing. This caused an increase in road traffic, creating problems for the swing bridge keeper at Litherland. In July 1894 the Clerk to the Local Board wrote complaining:

"The writer had occasion to call the attention of the person in charge of the bridge for detaining the traffic for a considerable period until there was an absolute block about a week ago, and we understand that on Saturday last the bridge was drawn for about twenty

The Iron Swingbridge at Litherland, installed in 1908. Liverpool Daily Post & Echo

The loaded barge Everton passes through Litherland Lift Bridge with Tommy Abrams steering.

minutes, and a considerable number of vehicles of all description were congregated on both sides of the canal, but in justice to the man on the bridge he did his best to close the same, but the people in charge of the boats would not stop to allow him to do so."[67]

He certainly seems to have been in a better mood than a month later when the Clerk again complained:

"On the writer coming to town on Saturday morning he observed this bridge drawn to permit of a canal boat passing through which was some distance away, and on the slope of the hill a heavily laden waggon was standing about six yards from the bridge, and it was with difficulty the horse could keep the waggon in position. The writer pointed out the absurdity of drawing the bridge and keeping a laden waggon standing within a few yards of the bridge and the only satisfaction he got from the canal company's caretaker was the abrupt reply 'You just mind your own business'"[68]

Crossing the canal here was to remain a problem, though the wooden bridge was replaced by an iron one in 1908, built in Garston by Francis Morton & Co. and carried by canal barge from Garston Docks to Litherland. The barge was ballasted, the bridge perching precariously on top of the gunwhales,[69] the overall clearance only just allowing passage through the bridge under Great Howard Street near Stanley Dock. A lifting bridge replaced the swing bridge in 1934, in its turn being demolished in the mid-seventies when a new overbridge was constructed to improve road access to the Royal Seaforth Dock.

In 1900 there were still a few open fields near Linacre Gas Works.[70] This had been opened in 1867 and was to become one of the largest in the area. Its reliance on the canal for supplies was reduced during the First World War when two carburetted water gas plants were opened which used imported oil as their raw material. However, gas was still produced from coal in part of the plant into the nineteen-sixties.

The chemical industry remained active in the area. There was an alkali factory next to the gas works and a soap works almost opposite. Adjoining this was a sack and bag works, the first of several near the canal. There was also Bootle's manure wharf and Pine Grove destructor, refuse being dispatched to West Lancashire by Corporation-owned canal boats even after the Second World War. Just after Strand Road bridge there were Appleby's corn mills. The firm, based at Enfield, near Accrington, had several other mills in East Lancashire and owned a large fleet of boats for carrying grain to them from the docks.

An aerial view of Linacre Gas Works, probably c1930. Bootle's Pine Grove destructor and Williams Toffee Works can be seen alongside the canal in the bottom of the photo. City Engineer's Department, Liverpool City Council.

There were few boat-yards on this section of the canal probably because shipwrights were always in great demand in Liverpool. Most canal boats used in Liverpool were built or repaired in West Lancashire where wages were lower and jobs scarcer. There was, however, a boat-yard in Canal Street, near Coffee House Bridge, operated for many years by the Skinners. Another, at the terminal basin, disappeared when Pall Mall was built. In the nineteen-thirties a new one opened when Parkes converted an arm at Bankhall into a dry-dock for the use of their coal boats, and this continued in use until coal traffic ceased in 1964.

Around the boundary between Bootle and Liverpool numerous terraced houses had been built by 1900, many on roads leading up to the canal, and footbridges crossed the canal to provide easy access to them.

Jarvis Robinson Transport Limited

28 BRUNSWICK STREET
LIVERPOOL

Phone—Bank 1274 (5 lines)

Branch Offices—

501 CLEVELAND STREET	ASHBURTON RD., TRAFFORD PARK
BIRKENHEAD	MANCHESTER
Phone—Birkenhead 2094	Phone—Trafford Park 58

*Shipping and Forwarding Agents
Cartage and Haulage Contractors*

View of Canal Wharf, Stables and Yard

1 CANAL STREET (MILLERS BRIDGE) BOOTLE

Phone Bootle 135

Canal Depot of JARVIS ROBINSON TRANSPORT LIMITED
28 BRUNSWICK STREET, LIVERPOOL.

Canal Street Wharf is conveniently situated for the important North End Docks and is specially adapted for the reception and despatch of Canal Traffic.

Jarvis Robinson's Wharf at Millers Bridge c1930. John Goodchild collection.

There was an abundance of small works as well. Amongst these were several timber yards including a clog sole and wood fibre factory in Ensor Street and a match factory on the opposite canal bank. Both needed regular supplies of timber. Numerous warehouses had been built alongside the canal as well, but it is uncertain if their trade relied on boats. There was another chemical works at Bankhall with R.S. Hudson's dry soap works opposite the canal warehouse, while on the other side of the bridge was Bankhall Oil & Chemical Works.

Through the railway bridge the North Corporation Yard had been built, where rubbish and manure were loaded into boats and railway waggons for delivery to West Lancashire farms. On the site next door, originally the Derby Coal-yard, a printing and carton making factory was opened in 1904 for the long established Bolton printing firm of John Tillotson.[71] Cartons were printed, cut and folded largely for the tobacco industry. Their main customer was the British and American Tobacco Company whose large factory was to be found alongside the canal between Sandhills Lane and Boundary Street. This site had been the Vauxhall Gardens before a variety of foundries and corn mills took over. All, with the exception of Bee Mills on Boundary Lane, were demolished for the new factory. Tillotson's was extended in 1934, at which time two thirds of its production was for the cigarette trade, though soap and food

Refuse being loaded at Sandhills Wharf c1900. Liverpool Libraries.

Tillotson's Cardboard Works can be seen on the right with BAT's Works beyond the bridge. Sandhills 1973. Philip Watkinson.

The dumb flat Heathdale being unloaded at Bee Mills, Sandhills after bringing goods through the docks.

packaging demands were increasing. The factory is one of the many to have been closed and demolished recently. At Boundary Street the Liverpool North Shore Rice and Flour Mills were still in production, while at Athol Street there was a new development, the works of the Liverpool Hydraulic Power Company, erected about 1885.[72] Steam driven pumps pressurised water, which was circulated through the centre of the city by underground mains. 4d per 1000 galloons was paid for canal water to fill the hydraulic mains and the Canal Companies annual standard charge of 10 shillings per engine horsepower for condensing water, used to increase engine efficiency by condensing exhaust steam. The company provided hydraulic power for lifts, presses and a variety of other uses for many years, closing down in 1970.

Former pumping station of the Liverpool Hydraulic Power Company on Athol Street. The Building is now the Liverpool Watersports Centre. The bridge was one of several over the canal in Liverpool enlarged early in the 20th century.

Nearer the town centre there were more changes, with warehousing, bottling stores, flour and oil mills having been established. At Burlington Street we come to Tate's sugar refinery. Henry Tate,[73] son of a Chorley Unitarian minister, had come to Liverpool in 1832 to learn the grocery trade. By 1859 he had six shops. To expand his interests he became a partner in John Wright's sugar refinery, selling his shops two years later. In 1869 the partnership was dissolved, Tate continuing alone and building a modern new refinery in Love Lane, backing onto the canal. It opened in 1872 to become one of the country's most successful refineries, being continually expanded as land and opportunity allowed. In 1921 the firm amalgamated with Abram Lyle & Sons of Greenock to become Tate and Lyle, subsequently taking over the Liverpool firms of Fairrie & Co. in 1929, and Macfie & Co. in 1938. The acquisition of other industrial sites in the area enabled the company to develop their works until it occupied both banks of the canal. One of those leased, in

Eldon Street

1950, was that of the Corporation's Burlington Street open air baths. Perhaps these did not pay as many lads preferred to go "skinny dipping" in the canal. When the terminal basin was abandoned in 1960, this too was partly taken over and developed, a new warehouse being built on the filled in bed of the canal. However, following the decline in use of sugar cane as a raw material the works have closed and been demolished, the Eldon Street housing development now occupying much of the site.

By 1900 most of the industry near the basin had declined, while the Corporation destructor and its chimney, demolished in the nineteen-fifties, dominated the surroundings. The Corporation was also responsible for the electricity station built on Pumpfields to supply the new electric trams. The moral welfare of the neighbourhood was catered for by All Souls Church, opened in 1856. A school was built alongside later. Today much has disappeared; only the generating station remains of the larger buildings and even that is likely to be demolished while this booklet is at press.

5
A Public Asset

The building of the canal was financed privately and it was to remain private property until nationalisation at the end of 1947. Even then the tow-path did not become a public right of way, and it was not until recently that it has become legal to use it as a footpath. From the earliest days there were problems with people trespassing. In 1777 the company minutes noted:

> "Whereas several complaints have been lately, made by the owners of land contiguous to the said canal navigation, of great damages being committed by disorderly, idle people breaking down the fences, destroying the herbage of the land, and fishing in the canal. Also by persons riding upon the towing path and turning cattle loose upon the banks contrary to the Act..."[74]

Notices were printed to confirm that the canal was private property, but the public continued to ignore them. There were even occasions when horse drawn carriages were found using the tow-path in order to evade turnpike dues. The canal also continued to attract those bent on leisure and in 1790 there were further complaints:

> "... of unqualified persons drawing nets in the canal and of disorderly idle persons breaking down the banks and fences and drawing the clows under pretence of fishing..."[75]

The Canal Company was concerned about interference with the water supply, but it was the land owners who complained about fishing as in the Canal's Act they were entitled to any fish caught.

The problem resulted from the ease of access to the tow-path, every bridge providing an unobstructed way of entry. Swing bridges were built originally, but over the years these were replaced by stone arches. When the canal was first built there were only seven bridges between the basin and Litherland, more being installed as the area developed.[76] Between Litherland and the Old Roan, where the swing bridge was replaced in 1787, the opposite has happened. Originally several occupation bridges were provided to link farm property divided by the construction of the canal. Most have now disappeared, the sale of fields isolated by the canal making them unnecessary. On these occupation bridges gates were sometimes provided to stop cattle wandering onto the tow-path.

The bridges could also be a problem if boatmen failed to close them. The Earl of Sefton complained to the Canal Company in 1803[77] that the bridge at Aintree which he used to reach home was often left open, causing him great inconvenience. Ever anxious to appease the local aristocracy, a cottage was built by the Company at a cost of £53 and Handcock, a canal employee, installed to look after the bridge, which is now known as Handcock's Bridge.

Access to the tow-path at the basin was unrestricted, and particularly easy from Old Hall Street. Following the building of Clarke's Basin there were several drownings late at night. To overcome the problem the Company fixed a chain around the water's edge which was removed during the day when boats were loading and unloading, and replaced at night to prevent accidents. The Company also provided lamp brackets, though they asked the local Commissioners of Watch, Scavenging and Lights to provide the lamps.[78]

Trespass on the tow-path in Liverpool was to remain a problem. In 1916 the Company replied to a request by the Corporation for gates controlling access to the canal at Chisenhale, Burlington, Lightbody, Athol, Boundary and Bankhall Streets and at Sandhills Lane, enquiring whether the gates should be solid or of open construction so that the police could see onto the tow-path. They noted that:

"The bridges which are the property of the Corporation with in some cases open and comparatively low parapets are a source of trouble to those using the canal and for the protection of boatmen and others the Company ask that the Corporation should erect closed parapets not less than five feet high, in order to prevent mischievous children from throwing missiles at passing horses and boatmen as is now the case. The gravel boxes especially that at Bankhall Bridge should also be removed further away from the canal as they supply ammunition for boys and others to throw at passing boats and much gravel is thus deposited in the canal."79

The gravel would have been used to help horse drawn traffic pass over the canal bridge in icy weather.

Gates seem to have been fitted about 1930, presumably fastened with the Canal Company's handcuff lock which would allow any company employee or boatman to open them. Someone must have left Lightbody Street gate unlocked in 1933 when a teacher from St. Sylvester's School took a party of children along the tow-path to reach the lock fields which they used for games. This had been forbidden as it encouraged children to use the tow-path. The school later apologised to the Company explaining that the teacher was new and was unaware that he was trespassing.

To prevent the tow-path becoming a right of way the Company observed a "halfpenny day" each year when every one using the tow-path was charged that amount for the privilege. The money was collected by the maintenance men, receipts being given after 1903 to avoid trouble, as on one occasion previously two old ladies had started to beat one of the men with their umbrellas as they thought he was begging. The custom died out about 1920 when cast iron notices were fixed forbidding cycling and trespassing. These slowly disappeared and were replaced by printed ones pasted up once a year.

Although the canal had always been an attraction and a danger spot for children, public concern about safety increased in the late nineteen-fifties as traffic declined. Bootle Corporation installed life-saving equipment in 1958 though it was continually vandalised. 1964 saw the end of coal deliveries to the gas works and three years later the section from Old Roan to Liverpool was closed to commercial traffic. Twenty-six children had been drowned there over the previous twelve years and there was a strong campaign by local MPs to have the canal filled in and

Angelo fitted with a grandstand at Aintree for races c1960. John Gibbons.

converted into a road to the docks. It would have been too expensive and nothing was done, though there were several reports produced on access and safety. As slum clearance took effect the problem moved further out to the new housing estates at Ford and Netherton. They were erected with little thought to the canal running through their centre and it was isolated by high fences. Today there is a more enlightened attitude which encourages the use of the tow-path by adults whose presence can restrain children. Pleasure boats are again beginning to use the canal into Liverpool, but years of problems with vandalism have given this section a bad name amongst boaters. Things were different when the canal first opened.

Packet boats, for the carriage of passengers and small items of goods, seem to have commenced between Liverpool and Wigan almost as soon as the canal opened. The Company charged one half penny for every two miles travelled by each passenger which allowed fourteen pounds weight of luggage free.[80] The bookkeeping associated with the packets may have proved difficult as the following year they were charged a single fee of £90 per annum per boat. There were two operators, Longbotham & Co., and the Union Company whose boat was owned by Messrs. Chadwick & Co. In 1776 another operator, Mr. Ellison, commenced operations, his tolls being at the old rate of a farthing per person per mile. A cheap rate of a half penny per return trip was introduced the same year for passengers travelling from Liverpool to Crosby Races.

Trips to the races, which became a regular feature of packet boat operation, reflect the intense local interest in sport. In the eighteenth century the Corporation maintained its own kennel of hounds for hunting,[81] and for many years these were between the canal and the foreshore near Bank Hall. Ormskirk Races were also served, return tickets in 1808 costing 1s.6d. in the fore cabin and 1s.0d. in the back. Aintree Race-course developed right alongside the canal. Originally there was no fence on the canal bank so many people used to watch the racing from boats or the tow-path. In 1924 the King watched the race from there with Lord Derby, who later thanked the Canal Company for organising this.[82] It must have alerted the Tophams, the course owners, to a source of lost revenue as the following year they leased the canal bank, though it was not until the nineteen-fifties that they erected a fence. Although stopping the view from the tow-path, people still came by boat for the Grand National, and several of the local carrying firms fitted

HACKINS-HEY.—Robert Gill, Carrier, leaves every Wednesday and Saturday for Ormskirk, Scarisbrick, and Burscough.

MITRE INN, Dale-street.—Carriers leave here every Tuesday and Friday for Preston and Leyland.

LEEDS AND LIVERPOOL CANAL PACKETS
BETWEEN LIVERPOOL, WIGAN, AND MANCHESTER.

Summer Season.—On and after the 1st of May, a Packet-boat will leave Liverpool for Wigan and Manchester, every morning at six o'clock.

Another Packet also leaves Manchester for Wigan and Liverpool at a quarter-past six.

The Boat from Liverpool will arrive at Scarisbrick-bridge at a quarter-before eleven in the morning, at Wigan at a quarter-before three in the afternoon, at Leigh at a quarter-past four, and at Manchester at a quarter-past eight in the evening.

The Boat from Manchester will arrive at Leigh at a quarter-past nine, Wigan at a quarter-before twelve in the morning, at Scarisbrick-bridge at four in the afternoon, and at Liverpool at half-past eight in the evening. Carriages attend the packets at Scarisbrick, to convey passengers to Southport, where they arrive at half-past eleven in the forenoon, and at five in the afternoon; thus providing a daily communication between the above places and Southport.

The extra Boat will leave Liverpool for Bootle, Linacre, and Crosby, every day at eight and ten in the morning, at half-past one and four in the afternoon, and at eight in the evening, except Sunday, on which day it leaves Liverpool at nine in the morning, at half-past one in the afternoon, and at seven in the evening.

Winter Season.—On and after the 1st of October, a Packet-boat leaves Liverpool for Wigan every morning at eight. Another Packet-boat leaves Wigan for Liverpool every morning at eight, each arriving at their respective destinations, at five in the evening.

A Packet-boat leaves the Old Roan at seven in the morning, every day except Sunday, and arrives at Liverpool at nine in the morning.

The same Packet leaves Liverpool on return to the Old Roan at four in the evening.

A Packet-boat in the Winter Season from Manchester, every day at seven in the morning, arrives at Wigan at twelve at noon, and departs thence at two in the afternoon, on its return to Manchester, where it arrives at seven in the evening.

RATES AND FARES IN THE CANAL PACKETS.

FROM LIVERPOOL	Front.	Back
To Bank-hall Bridge and Bootle	0s 6d	0s 4
Orrell and Linacre	0 8	0 6
Litherland	0 8	0 6
Crosby	1 0	0 6
Ford	1 3	0 10
Aintree	1 8	1 1
Maghull	2 8	1 9
Scarisbrick	3 0	2 0
Burscough	3 6	2 6
Appley Bridge	3 6	2 6
Wigan	5 6	3 6
Leigh	6 0	4 0
Worsley	6 0	4 0
Manchester	6 0	4 0
From Bootle and Crosby to Manchester	4 0	2 6
Scarisbrick, do.	2 6	1 3
Wigan, do.	1 10	1 3
Leigh, do.	1 8	1 0
Astley, do.	1 4	0 8
Worsley, do.	0 10	0 6
Barton, do.		

Intermediate distances in proportion.

Notice of times and fares for the packet boats, 1832.

grandstands to their boats for the occasion. Today the tradition continues and there are always a few pleasure boats in attendance on race day.

The Company took over the operation of the packets in 1782 after the Union Co. had found it difficult to make them pay in winter. They seem to have been built with two cabins divided by a kitchen in the centre which served food to the first class passengers in the fore cabin. There was accommodation on the roof, used in fine weather or when the cabins were full. The boats were usually well over 60 feet in length, though, in 1814, as the completion of the canal approached, a new packet was ordered specifically 62 feet long by 9 feet beam, so as to be capable of working through the short locks in Yorkshire.[83] Jonathan Blundell and Sons were the operators from 1789 and the following year Henry Blundell also ran a market boat between Halsall and Liverpool twice a week. From 1805 the Company again took back their operation, introducing new services over the next few years. From 1808 they operated daily to Wigan, with a market boat between Old Roan and Liverpool commencing in 1811. More trips were introduced on this service from 1813, providing a commuter service for the growing number of merchants living in Bootle and Litherland.

Bretherton's provided the horses, being paid £900 annually, and there were stables at Maghull, Burscough and Wigan. In Liverpool a covered dock was built to protect the packets, when they were not working, opposite Old Hall Street quay. It was from this quay that they operated, a bell being rung fifteen minutes before departure to ensure that everybody was aboard. Two horses pulled each boat, a rider on one blowing a horn to announce their coming and to urge on the horses. The packets continued to operate until the eighteen-forties when railways quickly took their custom.

As the nineteenth century progressed people had more spare time and by the eighteen-nineties there were several boat houses for pleasure craft erected near the residential area around Litherland. The Company charged a nominal sum for pleasure boats, though they were still subject to tolls when they passed through locks. 1932 saw the formation of the Mersey Motor Boat Club, who acquired canalside moorings at Litherland. With the post-war increase in leisure, they built a club house adjacent to their new moorings at Lydiate, further moorings being provided at Scarisbrick in the mid-nineteen-fifties. By 1972 when a study group on the development of the canal reported,[84] there were two rowing clubs near the Litherland tannery and the Sea Cadets had premises next to the boat club moorings.

The report suggested that it was hoped to establish a floating youth club at Lightbody Street. One of the boats which became available with the demise of the Wigan power station traffic was purchased and the author towed the boat into Liverpool. Unfortunately the project proved abortive, though more recently a water sports centre has been established in the old hydraulic pumping station at Athol Street. Other recent activity on the length has been the trip boat *Ambush* operated by Mike Sampson, while the local Inland Waterways Association members have a regular campaign cruise to Stanley Dock.

Access to the canal has always been difficult, and while much of the water supply came from the heavily polluted River Douglas there was little encouragement for recreational use. The poor quality of water deterred anglers. Over the past two decades there have been considerable improvements resulting in increased numbers of fish while cleaner water makes the tow-path a more attractive place.

6
What Future For Liverpool's Canal?

The future for this Remainder section of canal looks brighter today than some years ago when everyone from local residents to government departments seemed determined to turn their backs upon it. In 1966 the MP for Bootle, Simon Mahon, presented the canal as a potential route for Bootle's Dock Link road – after its infilling of course.

The Remainder Length, so called because government legislation during the nineteen-sixties declared it, along with several other waterways, to be of neither commercial nor cruising status, is eight miles long and runs from the Old Roan in Aintree to the Stanley Dock branch and the canal's present terminus at Burlington Street.

Where local authorities such as the County Borough of Bootle once argued for the canal's closure and infilling, both at a local and parliamentary level, the climate has changed today, and many organisations are now strongly committed to the rejuvenation of this long underused stretch of waterway. British Waterways, the controlling body for most of

Recreational use of the canal is not a new idea, but this one British Waterways are not seeking to promote! Liverpool Library.

Britain's inland waterway system, has frequently been criticised for its apparent neglect of some remainder waterways. Unfortunately the very status of remainder canals places constraints on spending and British Waterways have, in the past, been able to do little more than maintain minimum safety standards on some canals. However, recent organisational changes throughout British Waterways are now facilitating improvement schemes and new developments along many urban canals and the opportunity has arisen to breathe new life into Liverpool's canal. The restoration of remaining canalside buildings and the sensitive development of vacant sites, such as the Carolina Street wharf in Bootle, could provide the key to the successful regeneration of the canal.

The Wigan Pier development is an example of successful canalside regeneration. These former derelict warehouses are now a major tourist attraction.

If there is a vision for the future of Liverpool's canal then it is one of a canal wholly accepted by the people living around it. For more than a hundred years the people of Bootle and Vauxhall were the lifeblood of the canal - working on or beside this once busy waterway. When it no longer served the purpose for which it was built, the canal began a down turn, a black period when few were interested in it. Of those few who were concerned, British Waterways and the Inland Waterways Association were among the most active in the battle to safeguard the canal. Preventing its infilling was, until recently, all that could be done in terms of securing a future for the canal and although various bodies, including the Merseyside Civic Society in 1967, produced reports on the canal and its potential, there was perhaps insufficient funding or inclination to improve actively an environment that was becoming increasingly rundown and neglected.

Today, however, the vision is beginning to take shape. Right along the length of the canal initiatives are springing up which suggest that in the not too distant future, the canal will once again be a busy waterway, well used and appreciated by locals and perhaps increasingly by visitors. It is not expected, and may not even be desirable, that the Remainder Length becomes the home of a second Wigan Pier. Although that development has proved successful and is attracting thousands of visitors a year, what is needed on the Remainder Length at present is not tourist attractions but local amenities which will encourage those of us living near the canal to enjoy it to the full.

A successful regeneration of the canal will largely involve local people and local initiatives, some of which are already happening. As an example, in 1990 Sefton Council opened access points on to the canal towpath in Bootle Town centre, where none existed previously. The canal walkway scheme, as it is known, aims to encourage local use of the waterway and to help the canal shake off its "dirty old town" image. While no one wishes to destroy what remains of the canal's historical character, this can, of course, be better appreciated in a cleaner and pleasanter environment.

Further down the canal the influence of the Merseyside Development Corporation is also helping to secure a better future for the waterway. The MDC is currently the planning authority for the area around the last portion of the canal: from the Bootle boundary at Bedford Place to the lock flight and Burlington Street. The Development Corporation's regeneration strategy for the area involves extensive clearance of the industrial and derelict sites around the canal and, through the development of new housing and a business park, a complete facelift for the area. The proposed housing is to extend northwards from the successful Eldonian scheme which stands on a portion of the canal, infilled in 1987 following the closure of Tate and Lyle. Specific plans have yet to be drawn up, but proposals have been laid down and local people have been asked for their views. It seems almost certain that the potential for an attractive canalside development, one which acknowledges the waterway rather than turns its back on it, will at last be realised.

Ten years ago this housing in Litherland would certainly have been built with barbed wire and high railings along the canal edge.

With almost a thousand boats on the Leeds and Liverpool canal one might expect improvements to attract a flotilla of boats along the Remainder Length. The canal, however, is only just recovering from the last twenty or so years, when for many boaters a cruise into Liverpool was known as the equivalent of a journey to hell and back, due to the amount of rubbish in the canal and the number of projectiles hurled at boaters along the route. Happily the situation today is greatly improved and a trip down the Remainder Length and back is the annual campaign cruise of the local branch of the Inland Waterways Association. (To be fair, they are a group that have never given up on Liverpool's canal and have stalwartly carried on cruising in order to keep the length open). There are at present no moorings on this section of the canal, but it is to be hoped that more boaters will use it. Great numbers are not expected but the presence of boats will certainly contribute to an improved image for the canal.

The Greening of the Canal

Environmental issues are currently gaining a higher profile in everyone's mind, so the climate is ideal for getting people to think about their own environment and ways of improving it. Many volunteers, local groups and school children have become involved in canal related projects over the last few years. Projects include tree and bulb planting, clearance of waste ground next to the canal and improvements to access points. The involvement of local people working together with local authorities and British Waterways has made these sorts of projects easier to undertake, while they have been more successful precisely because of local interest and involvement from the outset.

It is not only the voluntary sector that is concerned with the "greening" of the canal. The MDC and MANWEB are committed to the removal of the numerous overhead gantries that follow the line of the canal for several miles from the top of Stanley Locks to the Rimrose Valley in Litherland. The removal of gantries will be a considerable environmental improvement and will also encourage anglers to use the length, which has its fair share of fish despite the bin bags and shopping trolleys which also find their way into the canal. British Waterways WATERWITCH spends almost 52 weeks of the year on the Remainder Length removing rubbish and weeds and helping to shake off the image of decay and neglect the canal has carried for so long. Businesses too have to be

The summer of 1991 saw the dismantling of the many overhead gantries along the canal. The power supply carried by the gantries has been re-routed underneath the roads.

encouraged to present a tidy face to the canal. Scenes of barbed wire, tumbledown walls and shoddy fencing are no longer acceptable if the canal is to be cleaned up and receive a new lease of life.

So, what should we expect for the future of the Remainder Length of the Leeds and Liverpool Canal? It is unlikely that it will be awarded cruising status, though that may be a long term aim of the authorities involved in its regeneration. What we can hope to see is a green and pleasant waterway lined with houses and businesses that relate to the canal, not turn away from it. Also a towpath that is used safely by walkers, cyclists and people on their way to work. Anglers and boaters may return

Clearing the canal of rubblish and weeds is a year-round job for British Waterways' Waterwitch.

to the length and community-based activities such as watersports, walks and fun events will increase along a canal that is no longer an eyesore but an asset. In effect the canal will have come full circle as the industry which it generated on its banks has grown and then fallen into decline and what we are left with is a thread of countryside weaving its way into the city as the canal in 1770 threaded its way through the agricultural land of Aintree, Litherland, Bootle and Vauxhall.

Appendix
Tow-path Remains

Much of the industry and warehousing which lined the canal has now disappeared together with the poorer quality housing in Bootle and Central Liverpool. However, there is still much to see on a walk along the tow-path.

After crossing the valley of the River Alt by a large embankment there is the site of a dredging tip where much of the mud removed from this section of the canal was dumped. The house built for Handcock, the

Caterick, built in 1952 for British Waterways, passing Browns Lane swing bridge at Netherton in the mid-nineteen-fifties. The steam tug '56' in the background was used for towing dredging spoil to the tip. Liverpool Daily Post.

bridge keeper, was removed when this tip was formed.[1] Around the corner can be seen Aintree Race-course. Originally it was created on the Liverpool side of Melling Road Bridge and was enlarged subsequently.[2] Before the Old Roan Bridge, where the former Preston Turnpike crossed the canal, is the industrial site first suggested in the early nineteen-twenties for businesses which wanted to move out of Liverpool.

Past Old Roan we enter the remainder stretch of waterway. Maintenance of this length has a lower priority than the upkeep of the rest of the canal. At Netherton we encounter the housing estates built during the Bootle slum clearances of the fifties and sixties. Lunar Drive, Apollo Way and Aldrins Lane, the first roads encountered here, all indicate the time of their construction.[3] After passing through the housing estate we reach Gorsey Lane. Just before the bridge is the wharf where many boats were loaded during the Second World War. It was built to save goods and boats from bomb damage in the docks.[4]

The canal now enters Rimrose Valley which was used as a tip for Liverpool's refuse,[5] the land on the tow-path side having been raised

Sewer being laid under the canal in 1954 during the construction of Netherton Housing Estate. Authors collection.

The approach to Litherland 1973 before the lifting bridge was replaced. Philip Watkinson.

considerably as a result. The buildings used by Litherland Tannery remain on the offside, two egg ended boilers at the north end, probably dating from early last century, being converted into storage tanks.[6] Just past the tannery is a winding hole in the far canal bank which enabled boats delivering here to turn round. These were provided at many places along the canal which was usually narrower than the 60 or 70 foot long boats normally used. Other regular features found on the towpath are ramps, sometimes covered with removable wooden planks, which allowed the rescue of boat horses which had fallen in the canal, a not uncommon occurrence.

Entering Litherland the canal is crossed by the new bridge carrying traffic to and from the docks. Just beyond is the narrows where the lift bridge and its swinging predecessor were located. The bridge keeper's house remains, as does the footbridge first provided in 1908.[7] The tar distillery on the offside is a reminder of the chemical industry so long associated with the canal in Liverpool.[8]

Passing under the railway bridge carrying the branch from Bootle to Aintree there are several factories on the offside including a tannery

Everton is famous for toffee, but it was also made in Bootle, Williams'
factory is seen here from the Strand Bridge. Opposite is Linacre Gas
Works while beyond was Bootle's manure wharf.

built c1890, while beyond Pennington Road Bridge is the remains of a
lead works dating from the turn of the century.[9] Linacre Gas Works is
reached after the next bridge, and the tow-path wall reveals several
bricked up doorways where coal was delivered and gas tar removed by
boat.[10] The gas works continued beyond Marsh Lane Bridge as far as
Litherland Road. On the opposite bank is the site of the Pine Grove destructor where Bootle's rubbish was dealt with, much of it being
removed by boat.[11] Next door is William's Toffee Factory, with its
chimney dating from 1911.[12] Litherland Road bridge, rebuilt in 1887,
still has evidence of the vertical rollers used to stop boat hauling lines
from wearing against the bridge structure.

A frosty day on the canal showing the site of Bootle Warehouse, demolished in the early nineteen-eighties.

At Stanley Road Bridge the tow-path changes side. The reason for this usually dates back to the period when horses pulled boats and the strain tended to pull them towards the canal. Change line bridges such as this allowed the strain to be reversed, giving some respite to the horse. Here, however, the reason is to stop access from the tow-path to the former Canal Company warehouse and arm at Carolina Street,[13] the tow-path again changing sides before the railway bridge near Oriel Road Station is reached. The iron stump on the wharf is the remains of a crane used to unload boats.

Coffee House Bridge is next, with the Dundee sacking works located on the offside a couple of hundred yards beyond.[14] From here to Bankhall the canal passes a variety of buildings, mainly housing as far as Millers Bridge on the tow-path side, with the remains of industrial building on the offside. Warehousing appears beyond the bridge, though

Coffee House Bridge during reconstruction in the mid-nineteen-thirties. The two coal boats are probably going to unload at Linacre Gas Works. They may have been loaded from railway wagons at Sandhills as they are proceeding in the opposite direction to that normally taken by loaded boats. Perhaps there was a stoppage on the canal between Wigan and Liverpool. Liverpool Daily Post & Echo.

the mix of housing and commerce remains virtually to Bankhall Bridge.[15] On the offside, 250 yards before the bridge can be seen the Caledonia Foundry and Engine Works. The Canal Company's warehouse alongside the bridge dates from the eighteen-seventies and straddled a short arm, but this has now been filled in and the entrance bricked up. There is also a covered wharf where goods could be transshipped in the dry. This wharf became the base for John Parke and Sons who converted an arm into a dry-dock for their boats in the mid-nineteen-thirties. The firm was the last to carry coal into Liverpool and were also involved in the manure traffic. Their fleet of boats was purchased by British Waterways shortly before the coal traffic ceased. On the tow-path side of the canal opposite the wharf are a collection of warehouses and industrial buildings. In particular there is Hudson's Soap Works next to the bridge, another reminder of Liverpool's chemical industry. The

Little now remains of the North Manure Wharf at Sandhills but the loading platforms indicate where it was located.

buildings to the north of Bank Hall Bridge have not yet been made subject to widespread demolition, and give the best impression of the former importance of the canal corridor to Liverpool's industrial base.

Beyond Bankhall Bridge, after passing the site of Canada Dock Goods Yard, we soon reach the railway bridge carrying the former Lancashire and Yorkshire Railway over the canal. Water to supply locomotives in their engine shed at Bankhall was taken from the canal just before this bridge. Transshipping facilities may have been provided here as well. They certainly were just through the bridge where the remains of a manure loading wharf can be seen.[16] Tillotson's cardboard box factory was located behind this wharf, occupying the space up to Sandhills Bridge. The entrance gateway is all that remains. Opposite, against the tow-path, are the oil and turpentine works of Banner & Co.

After the bridge are the remains of Bee Mills, used as warehousing for many years. They eventually passed to the British American Tobacco Company Limited whose works extend from here almost to Boundary Street.[17] The tow-path here overlooks the former site of Huskisson Goods Depot. The North Shore Mills used to be next to Boundary Street Bridge which shows clear evidence of strengthening and widening. It has two distinct arches, one of stone and the other of iron.

Around Boundary Street there has been considerable demolition, though the hydraulic pumping station remains following its conversion to a water sports centre.[18] Between Athol Street and Lightbody Street is another gasworks site. Access for coal brought by boat was through doorways, now bricked up, some of which are fitted with cast iron surrounds to prevent damage. Beyond Lightbody Street Bridge the branch down to Stanley Dock leaves the canal's main line.[19] Little remains past the junction and the canal is now blocked at Burlington Street. This section remained in use until the 1960s, the concrete wharf opposite the branch dating from ten years earlier when it was hoped that the warehousing and carriage of tinned fruit would be developed there. Groceries were always one of the canal's main traffics, often delivered to Leeds, 127 miles away by canal as the mile-post near the top of the locks shows.

Across the entrance to the branch a pipeline now uses the footbridge supports which previously carried the tow-path. The site of the lock cottage near this bridge can also be seen. Walking down the locks note the paddle gear. Much is of an old pattern which has almost disappeared from the rest of the canal. There are also hooks fixed in the ground at the head of some of the locks. In horse boat days the tow-line was fastened to these, passing through a pulley on the boat's towing mast before leading to the horse. This halved the strain on the horse when pulling a boat out of the lock. The rope was eventually stopped from passing through the pulley by a peg in the line, which then slipped off the hook as the boat passed.

On the Lightbody Street side of the branch is the destructor operated by the Bootle Barge Company where they burn rubbish they remove from the docks, while below are several former wharfs originally built for the slate trade. The entrance to the Bridgewater Canal's basin, now filled in, is visible between the bottom lock and Great Howard Street

Bridge. Opposite is the pump house, built in the nineteen-thirties to return water used by the locks back to the main canal. The discharge point at the top of the locks is on the south side of the branch. The wool warehouse, built by the Dock Board around the turn of the century, was located between the railway viaduct and Great Howard Street. Some features remain visible in the tow-path wall, though the warehouse has been demolished.

Beyond Great Howard Street is Stanley Dock, where, for the time being a thriving Sunday market is held. The original warehouses were by Jesse Hartley and are generally similar to those at Albert and Wapping Docks. About a third of the north stack was destroyed in the Blitz while the south stack is hidden behind A.G. Lyster's enormous 1901 tobacco warehouse, which is built on an infilled portion of the dock. From numerous points on the flight of locks it is possible to see an hexagonal tower, about a quarter of a mile away: this is the Salisbury Clock, standing at the river entrance which served Stanley. In addition to twin half-tide gates, it has a small lock which enabled flats and those canal boats which had coamings and covers to enter or leave at more or less any state of the tide. The tower also contained a signal bell and a small flat for the Piermaster. Owing to the removal of redundant dock bridges it is now a very long walk indeed to Salisbury Entrance and permission must in any case be sought from the Mersey Docks and Harbour Company.

Left above: Coal being unloaded at Tate & Lyle's c.1960. The motor boat Jeanette has brought coal from Crooke, near Wigan. The other boats moved coal, brought by lorry, from one side of the canal to the other. This was necessary because of the confined nature of the site.

Left below: The former Bridge Inn, Burlington Street, a noted haunt of boatmen. It has "basement entrance" from the tow-path.

Above: The Canal Company's Warehousing on Pall Mall still stands, but while the basin dating from the eighteen-eighties is recognisable, as this recent photo shows, it was filled in the during the nineteen-sixties.

NOTES

Chapter 1

1. For more information about Thomas Steers see: Henry Peet, Thomas Steers, *Transactions of the Historic Society of Lancashire and Cheshire*, vol. 82 (1931) pp.162-241, and N. Ritchie-Noakes and Mike Clarke, *The Dock Engineers and the Development of the Port of Liverpool* in *Liverpool Shipping, Trade and Industry*, Liverpool 1989.

2. Longbotham was a Halifax man who had worked with John Smeaton on the Calder and Hebble Navigation. His work on the Leeds and Liverpool was probably undertaken for John Stanhope of Horsforth near Leeds. He worked on a number of other canal projects before his death, in poverty, in 1801.

3. Brindley was offered the post of Canal Engineer but rejected it because of pressure of work. His assistant Robert Whitworth seems to have undertaken the survey. Whitworth was called in several times for his advice before finally becoming engineer from 1793 virtually until his death in 1800.

4. Edward Baines, *A History of Liverpool*, Liverpool 1852.

5. Following the death of John Stanhope, Hustler became the canal's leading proprietor. He was a Quaker wool merchant from Bradford, becoming the canal's Treasurer in 1771, subsequently purchasing coal mines in the Douglas valley. He died in 1780.

6. Details relating to the rebuilding of the Douglas Navigation taken from the Liverpool Committee Minutes 1777-80, P.R.O. RAIL 846/42.

7. J.R. Ward, *The finance of canal building in eighteenth century England*, Oxford Historical Monographs, 1974.

8. P.R.O. RAIL 846/42, 21 March 1776.

9.   P.R.O. RAIL 846/42, 15 November 1775.

10.   Coamings are the upright edging boards around the hold of a boat to which the sheets covering the hold are fixed.

11.   Statistical history of the Leeds and Liverpool, P.R.O. RAIL 846/124.

12.   Packet boats only carried people and small packets of goods. They were often narrow beamed boats drawn by teams of horses which were changed regularly. Express cargo or flyboats were conventional cargo carrying barges operating to a set timetable or nonstop.

13.   Prior to the Canal Carriers Act of 1845 most canal companies had not been authorised to carry goods. Several canals did have fleets before this Act, but not the Leeds and Liverpool.

14.   Canals did not come under Government control until 1917, much later than railways. They also returned to private control earlier, a subsidy towards increased wartime costs only being paid during Government control. Thus canals received less financial help than railways.

Chapter 2

15.   Edward Baines, *op cit.*

16.   Land values in Liverpool were from 300 – 800 per acre as against £50 – £200 elsewhere on the canal. Land purchase book, P.R.O. Rail 846/119.

17.   The canal often purchased more land than was actually needed for its construction. Fields were divided by the canal and those parts which were uneconomic were sold to the company who thus became owners of much canalside property.

18.   P.R.O. RAIL 846/42, 28 October 1775.

19. Gibraltar was named after the eighteenth century battle, while Dutton was the name of the land owner.

20. Income from merchandise traffic in Lancashire rose from 34,597 in 1814 to 66,681 in 1818. By the time the Leigh branch had been open for three years, in 1823, merchandise income from Lancashire had reached 109,939.

21. Income from the Lancashire section (Liverpool to Wigan) of the canal was usually 50% above that for the Yorkshire section (Johnson's Hillock to Leeds) before railway competition began to affect the tolls in 1848. The Liverpool coal trade was probably the main reason for this: average journey distances of around 25 miles in Lancashire were twice those for Yorkshire.

22. Information from the Liverpool Medical Officer's Report of the Sub-committee on the causes of excessive mortality of the town. Evidence of Mr. Worsnop on conditions in Liverpool, given 12 May 1866.

23. Quoted in E.W.Hope, Evolution of Sanitation in Liverpool, 1844-1894. *Proceedings of the Liverpool Literary and Philosophical Society*, vol. 50, 1895/6, pp293-312.

24. A.L.M. Cook, *Liverpool's Northern Hospital*, Liverpool 1981.

25. Report of Mr. Arnold Taylor to the Secretary of State as to the alleged nuisance occasioned by the deposit of refuse at Phillips Street Wharf, 1866, p12.

26. Ibid, p.22.

27. P.R.O. RAIL 846/16, 8 April 1853.

28. Canal Company papers relating to the Liverpool and Bury Railway extension.

29. P.R.O. RAIL/124.

30. Ibid.

31. George Smith, 1831-95. Author of *Our Canal Population. A Cry from the Boat's cabin* published in 1875 in which he complained about conditions for boatmen's families on the narrow canals of the Midlands. As a result of his work two Acts were passed, in 1877 and 1884, regulating the living accommodation on board canal boats.

32. P.R.O. Home Office correspondence, MH 25/27, 6 March 1876.

33. Liverpool Record Office, 352 MIN/HEA 25/1-3.

34. H. Percy Boulnois, Refuse Destructors, *Transactions of the Liverpool Engineering Society*, vol. 13, 1891-92, pp.125-150.

35. W.A. Herdman ed., *Handbook to Liverpool and the Neighbourhood*, Liverpool 1896.

36. Lancashire R.O., Minutes of the Lancashire Farmers Union, Ormskirk, pp.135-41.

37. Quoted by Ernest Rosbottom, *Burscough — The Story of an Agricultural Village*, 1987, p.148.

38. *Handbook of the Congress of the Royal Institute of Public Health*, Liverpool, 1903.

39. Canal Company papers.

40. And even that will probably have been demolished while this book is at press.

Chapter 3

41. P.R.O. RAIL 846/2, 22 June 1774.

42. P.R.O. RAIL 846/42, 24 January 1775.

43. P.R.O. RAIL 846/42, 4 April 1776.

44. P.R.O. RAIL 846/42, April-May 1776.

45. Haigh MSS 23/6/190.

46. Canal Company papers.

47. Lancs. R.O. DP 175.

48. P.R.O. Rail 846/11, 29 January 1834.

49. John Goodchild Collection, Wakefield Library.

50. From plans in the Mersey Docks & Harbour Board Collection, Maritime Record Centre.

51. Doncaster R.O., Warde-Aldam Papers DDWa/N/5/3.

52. P.R.O. RAIL 846/24, 18 August 1892.

Chapter 4

53. An alkali is a material which tends to neutralise an acid.

54. Swing bridges were almost universal when the canal was built. They were only replaced by stone arch, iron or steel bridges as road traffic increased over the years.

55. The drinking of coffee became widespread during the eighteenth century. Coffee houses became important meeting places where news and business information were exchanged.

56. J.A. Picton, *Memorials of Liverpool*, London, 1873, p.85.

57. P.R.O. RAIL 846/42, 15 November 1775.

58. P.R.O. RAIL 846/16, 23 January 1850.

59. Picton, *op cit*, p468.

60. Details of Liverpool's gas works are taken from Stanley A. Harris, *The Development of Gas Supply on North Merseyside, 1815-1949*, Liverpool 1956.

61. Cannel is a bituminous coal, rich in gas, which has a low ash content.

62. Tom Jones, *Henry Tate*, 1819-1899, London 1960, p.11.

63. Information about James Muspratt and other Liverpool chemical manufacturers is from D.W.F. Hardie, *A History of the Chemical Industry in Widnes*, pp.10-24.

64. Ibid.

65. Canal Company papers.

66. Wakefield R.O., C299/156.

67. Canal Company papers.

68. Ibid.

69. A gunnel or gunwhale is the planking or plating covering the upper end of the framing of a boat. On barges they are used for access from one end of the boat to the other.

70. Harris, *op cit*.

71. Frank Singleton, *Tillotsons. 1850-1950*, Bolton and London 1950, pp.73-85.

72. Canal Company papers.

73. J.A. Watson, *A Hundred Years of Sugar Refining, Liverpool 1973*, pp.5-77.

Chapter 5

74. P.R.O. RAIL 846/42, 12 July 1777.

75. P.R.O. RAIL 846/44, 27 August 1790.

76. P.R.O. RAIL 846/42, 23 September 1777, list of bridges between Liverpool and Dean (Gathurst).

77. P.R.O. RAIL 846/47, 13 December 1803.

78. Picton, *op cit*, pp.42-3, and P.R.O. RAIL 846/43, 2 February 1792 and RAIL 846/45, 1 March 1798.

79. Canal Company papers.

80. For more information on packet boats see Mike Clarke, *The Leeds and Liverpool Canal, a History and Guide.*

81. Picton, *op cit*, p.365.

82. P.R.O. RAIL 846/34, 23 April 1924.

83. Packet boats usually worked between Liverpool and Manchester so could be up to 70 feet long. The *Blackburn Gazette* of 15th October 1834 reported that an iron boat of this length, weighing 4 tons and drawing 6 inches, had been built by Reid and Hanna in Liverpool for the canal luggage trade. The boat, which could carry 25 tons, was probably a new packet boat.

84. Leeds and Liverpool Canal, retention and improvement, report of the study group, May 1972.

BIBLIOGRAPHY

Sources

For those who want to know more about the Leeds and Liverpool, Mike Clarke's previous book about the canal contains a full list of the main sources of information. The only new material concerning the canal comes from Canal Company business records which are, unfortunately, not available to the public. Information on the canalside businesses has been gleaned from a variety of directories, many of which are available in the Local History Department of Liverpool City Libraries. Ordnance Survey and other maps of the area were also studied from which the development of the area can be traced. The Local History Library also provided much detailed information on the health of the town and on the improvements in sewage and refuse handling. This was supplemented at the Lancashire Record Office where details of the use of manure by West Lancashire farmers were located.

Donald Anderson, *The Orrell Coalfield, Lancashire, 1740-1850*, Moorland, 1975.

Edward Baines, *A History of Liverpool*, Liverpool 1852.

Gordon Biddle, 'The Leeds and Liverpool Canal', *Waterways World*, August 1981 and September 1981.

Gordon Biddle, *Pennine Waterway*, Dalesman, 1979.

Borough of Liverpool, Health Committee, *Improvements And Extension of the Canal Manure Wharfs*, Liverpool 1865.

H. Percy Boulnois, 'Refuse Destructors', *Transactions of the Liverpool Engineering Society*, vol. 13, 1891/2, pp.125-50.

Mike Clarke, *The Leeds and Liverpool Canal: a History and Guide*, Preston 1990.

A.L.M. Cook. *Liverpool's Northern Hospital,1834-1978*, Liverpool 1981.

A CURSORY view of a proposed canal from Kendal to the Duke of Bridgewater's Canal... with several proposals addressed to the proprietors of the Grand Canal between Leeds and Liverpool, 1769.

AN EXPLANATION of the plan of the canal from Leeds to Liverpool, Bradford, 1788.

Gary Firth, 'Bradford coal, Craven Limestone and the origins of the Leeds and Liverpool Canal, 1765-1775', *Journal of Transport History*, 3rd series, vol. VI, 1983.

Charles Hadfield and Gordon Biddle, *The Canals of North West England*, 2 vols., Newton Abbot 1970.

Handbook of the Congress of the Royal Institute of Public Health, Liverpool, 1903.

Handbook to Liverpool and the Neighbourhood, British Association, 1896.

John Hannavy and Jack Winstanley, *Wigan Pier: an Illustrated History*, Wigan 1985.

D.W.F. Hardie, *A History of the Chemical Industry in Widnes*, ICI, 1950.

John Raymond Harris, 'Liverpool Canal Controversies, 1769-1772', *Journal of Transport History*, vol. 2, 1956.

Stanley A. Harris, *The Development of Gas Supply on North Merseyside, 1815-1949*, Liverpool 1956.

Sir George Head, *A Home Tour through the Manufacturing Districts of England in the summer of 1835*, London 1836.

E.W. Hope, Evolution of sanitation – Liverpool, 1844-1894. *Proceedings of the Liverpool Literary and, Philosophical Society* vol. 50, 1895-96, pp.293-312.

Tom Jones, *Henry Tate, 1819-1899*, London 1960.

H.F. Killick, 'Notes on the early history of the Leeds and Liverpool Canal', *Bradford Antiquary*, n.s., vol. 2, July 1897.

John Langton, *Geographical Change and Industrial Revolution; Coalmining in South West Lancashire, 1590-1799*, Cambridge 1979.

Leeds and Liverpool Canal Company, *Official Handbook*, 1927.

Leeds and Liverpool Canal Company, *Twixt Leeds and Liverpool*, Liverpool 1936.

Leeds and Liverpool Canal, Retention and Improvement, Report of the study group, May 1972.

Tony Lewery, 'The Northern Tradition', *Waterways World*, June 1975.

James Newlands, *Liverpool, Past and Present in Relation to Sanitary Operations*, Liverpool 1859.

Edward W. Paget-Tomlinson, *Britain's Canal and Rivercraft*, Moorland 1979.

Edward W. Paget-Tomlinson, *The Complete Book of Canal and Riverside Navigations*, Waine Research Publications, 1978.

J.A. Picton, *City of Liverpool Municipal Archives and Records*, 1886

J.A. Picton, *Memorials of Liverpool*, London 1873.

Report of Mr. Arnold Taylor to the Secretary of State as to the alleged nuisance occasioned by the deposit of refuse at Phillips Street Wharf, Liverpool 1866.

Report of the sub-committee on the causes of excessive mortality of the town, Liverpool 1866.

Dr. Gordon W. Roderick and Dr. Michael D. Stephens, 'Profits and Pollution: Some problems facing the chemical industry in the nineteenth century. The Corporation of Liverpool versus James Muspratt, alkali manufacturer, 1838', *Industrial Archaeology*, vol. 11, no. 2, Spring 1974, pp.35-45.

Ernest Rosbottom, *Burscough; the Story of an Agricultural Village*, Preston 1987.

Frank Singleton, *Tillotsons, 1850-1950*, Bolton and London 1950.

A SUMMARY view of the proposed canal from Leeds to Liverpool, Bradford 1768.

J.A. Watson, *A Hundred Years of Sugar Refining*, Liverpool 1973.

Geoffrey Wheat, *Leeds and Liverpool Canal Craft*, 1972.

Arthur Young, *A Tour of the North Country*.

MIKE CLARKE: BIOGRAPHICAL DETAILS

Mike Clarke was born in Liverpool in 1948, and his secondary education was at the Liverpool Institute High School. He left in 1964 to serve his time as an apprentice fitter/turner with Pilkington Brothers at St. Helens, at the same time obtaining an ONC and HND in Mechanical Engineering. Always interested in transport history, vintage cars became his daily transport, and he became a part owner of a steam railway engine for a short time. At Birmingham University, he discovered canals and realised that it was possible to earn a living working on industrial restoration projects. The next fifteen years were engaged in rebuilding a wide variety of objects: canal boats to traction engines, colliery winding engines to flour mills. For five of these years he lived on board a wooden Leeds and Liverpool boat, travelling the canal and meeting many exboatmen. Following this he resolved to write a history of the canal when time became available. In 1980 he became engineer at the Helmshore Textile Museum in Lancashire, but after five years had to retire because of ill-health. To keep working he took a post in the local library at Accrington. In his spare time he then wrote the history of the Leeds and Liverpool Canal, published in 1990 and shortlisted for the Portico Book Prize.

ALLISON HEWITT: BIOGRAPHICAL DETAILS

Allison Hewitt was born in Liverpool in 1964. A graduate of Liverpool University, she has worked on the Leeds and Liverpool Canal since 1987.

As Project Officer for the Remainder Length of the canal, her work is to assist in the rejuvenation of the waterway through environmemtal improvements and also through the encouragement of educational and recreational projects.

Getting local people interested and involved in the canal is an essential part of the Project's work and to that end Allison regularly gives talks about and leads walks along the Leeds and Liverpool Canal. A recent seminar at Liverpool University was coordinated by Allison and focussed on urban canals in the North West.

The post of Project Officer is funded by British Waterways, Merseyside Development Corporation and Sefton Council.

Index

Chisenhale Street, 21, 37, 39, 53, 59, 72
Clarence Dock, 44
Clarence foundry, 59
Clarke's Basin, 26, 30, 39, 72
Clarke, Mr., 21
Coal, 9 - 10, 12, 14 - 17, 20 - 21, 28, 31, 36, 43, 45, 49 - 51, 55, 57, 59, 63 - 64, 73, 90, 92
Coal Dock, 42
Coal dust, 28
Coal gas, 10
Coal heavers, 22
Coal yards, 21
Coffee House Bridge, 54, 64, 89
Collingwood Dock, 34, 45
Commercial Road, 31
Copper, 9, 17, 50
Cotton, 17, 53
Crosby Races, 74
Crosfield, Barrow & Co., 56

Derby Dock, 43
Derby, Lord, 17, 74
Destructor, 34, 63 - 64, 70, 88, 92
Dickenson, Robert, 11
Diesel engines, 12
Dock Board, 48
Dock Committee, 20, 44 - 46, 48
Dock Dues, 45
Douglas Navigation, 7, 9 - 12, 14, 41
Duncan, Dr., 24, 26
Dutton Street, 20

Eagle, Mr., 41
East Lancashire Railway, 15, 28, 53
Eccles Street, 55
Eldon Street, 70

Eldonian development, 81
Ellison, Mr., 74
Ensor Street, 65 - 66

Fairrie, J.T. & A., 56, 59, 69
Flags, 45
Fletcher, Mr., 42
Flour, 57, 69
Ford, 74
Forrester, G., & Co., Messrs., 53

Gardner, R.P., & Co., 56
Garston Docks, 63
Gas, 55 - 56, 63, 73, 92
Gas lighting, 53
Gas works, 15 - 16
Gerard Bridge, 52
Glass, 14, 51 - 52
Glassware, 17
Gouthwaite and Moore, 57
Gouthwaite and Moore, Messrs., 52
Grain, 10
Grand National, 74
Great Howard Street, 12, 20, 28, 44, 63, 92 - 93

Hadfield, G., & Co, 49
Hadfield, Thomas, 59
Halewood family, 52
Halfpenny day, 73
Handcock's Bridge, 72
Harrington Dock, 27
Hartley, Jesse, 44, 93
Hill, William, 59
Howard, John, 20
Hudson, R.S., 66
Hustler and Co., 21
Hustler, John, of Bradford, 9
Hustler, Mr., 42